MW00770502

Praise from aroun‹
The Natural Laws of Management: The Admin Scale

Our company was operating for ten years without the Hubbard management technology. Then we were introduced to this engineering-precise tech. And what were the results? In the first ten years of our company we had grossed just over 5 million dollars with about 20 retail stores. Our market share was under 2%. At the end of the second ten years, utilizing these effective tools of management, the sales were 175 million dollars with more than 60 stores with a 20% market share.

Strikingly, we discovered that we were no longer totally dependent on "brilliant staff," as everything we do now is fully memorialized and the policies are consulted on a regular basis. They are the guiding principles that everyone in the company now follows.

The Natural Laws of Management: The Admin Scale provides a practical library of the key components and methodology we have used successfully in the expansion of our business.

Peter Fazekas
Managing Director, Euronics, Hungary

***

For me, time management was always a big issue. I am a civil engineer and I had a construction company which I considered was very difficult to manage. When I discovered and studied L. Ron Hubbard's management technology, I saw there were solutions to these problems. The application of the technology gave me new possibilities. Now I have three construction companies, a consulting company and a wellness company (a detox center) while I have more time for me, my family and my friends!!!

A vital part of this technology which helped me to stay focused and complete targets easier and faster is the alignment technology covered in this book.

Thank you for publishing this book. It will be a great help for the business world.

Giannis Bogdanos
Entrepreneur, Athens, Greece

As the founder of Performia, an international recruitment support organization, I wanted to quickly build an organization that could impinge all over the world and help businesses win faster through better and more effective hiring procedures. The Administrative Scale of Importance technology, as described in this book, has enabled us to build an organization operating today in 20 countries.

Before I knew this information I struggled quite a bit even though we had many great people employed. The problem was that staff were often acting and operating more or less out of alignment with goals, strategy, plans and policies and that created a lot of stress, lost time, lost money, less expansion and this was a bit upsetting to all of us. I had to solve many more problems with staff then than I do today even though we have more staff and they are a lot more spread out geographically than before. The real power of alignment should not be underestimated.

Arte Maren is a great speaker and experienced presenter of great ideas and in this book he provides an absolutely key tool to organizational as well as personal expansion. I always use it now and, as with all real true and great solutions, its simplicity and usefulness, once you really understand the component parts, make it second nature to you. You have in your hand the truth about personal and organizational alignment and expansion. If you simply study it and apply it, it will definitely work for you and your organization as well.

Marten Runow
CEO, Performia International, Sweden

***

This book is phenomenal! I hate to brag...but I have such a wonderful life and it is ALIGNED! And the data in your book IS the data I applied to have the great life I have – in my business, my marriage, as a parent and just as me – having time to do what I enjoy. I know this is rough for folks – juggling all the different aspects of life and making it all work, so I hope a ton of people buy, read and apply what you have written in *The Natural Laws of Management: The Admin Scale.*

Joy Gendusa, Founder/CEO, PostcardMania

The Natural Laws of Management: The Admin Scale is a much-needed book. The material not only provides enormous benefits for running a business successfully with hundreds of employees (as I have) but for correctly managing our large family of seven (five boys!). It is a must-read for any parent.

Ben Kugler, Founder & CEO of The Family Advisory

***

The information provided in Arte Maren's book, *The Natural Laws of Management: The Admin Scale*, is more valuable and more practical than any other management principles I have ever studied.

After an MBA completion at USC I almost bankrupted my business because I did not have down-to-earth tools to manage my way out of constant struggle. Then I discovered the technology of alignment and within a year I built a multi-million dollar consulting business. Our company is one of the biggest management consulting firms in Europe .

Thanks to the Hubbard management technology, we were ISO 9001 certified in 50% of the normal time.

Today we use and apply the tools in this book on a daily basis – with our clients and for ourselves – simply because it represents the foundation of any long-term stability and expansion.

Arte Maren is a master speaker and trainer. *The Natural Laws of Management: The Admin Scale* is an invaluable concentration of his experience and his expertise in the Hubbard management technology. It is also a great attestation of his unique ability to convey information in a way that you can immediately apply – and see the results faster than you can breathe! I have known Arte for over 15 years and I will attest that his great communication skills and his technical expertise make him one of my favorite speakers.

Thank you so much for this unique piece of art in the field of practical management.

Patrick V. Valtin, Clearwater, Florida
International speaker, trainer, entrepreneur and author of *New Era Selling: How to Win Bigger Sales in Saturated, Overly Competitive Markets*

Our company, MASCO Security Ltd, is the largest safety technology and gates automation dealer in Hungary. We have been representing European, Asian and American safety technology and gate automation products since 1992.

Our growth was not an easy process until we began using the Hubbard management technology that you have provided in this book. Using this technology gave us the ability to align all parts of our operation resulting in greater production. Overall, it allowed me to escape the common traps that many entrepreneurs experience and using these tools, we not only became the biggest in our industry in my country but it helped us to implement the ISO 9001 standards in a hyper fast speed.

I am very pleased to see the publication of your book *The Natural Laws of Management: The Admin Scale*, which will help other entrepreneurs and business owners to implement L. Ron Hubbard's management solutions so that they too may experience greater growth with less effort.

Juhos, Nándor (Mr.)
Executive Director, MASCO Security Ltd., ISO 9001
Budapest, Hungary

***

We are a manufacturing company of woodworking machinery. We have been in business for over 50 years in Modena, Italy. Prior to the introduction and utilization of Hubbard management technology the entire business was "personality driven." With the introduction of this powerful technology, the effort and stress has drastically reduced. Our accounts payable are completely handled because of the sound financial system and the increased income.

The Natural Laws of Management: The Admin Scale is a book I had hoped to see as I attended Arte Maren's presentation of this technology while he was on his speaking tour in Italy and I had many realizations about the business in general and especially about the important balance between personal and company goals. And, as far as growth is concerned, I am happy to report a 47% increase in sales over last year!

Valter Brignoli
Valerial Brignoli S.R.L. (Societa a responsabilita limitata)

The Natural Laws of Management: The Admin Scale is a must-read for any business owner, anyone who wants to own a business or an employee who wants to do a better job. It has been said, "The person without a plan will wind up somewhere." You don't want to wind up somewhere. So you need a plan. The vital information in Arte's book will not only help you develop a plan to help accomplish your dreams, you will be using the best data on Planet Earth on the subject of planning. Arte is a master of the planning technology developed by L. Ron Hubbard. With Arte's book, you can develop your plan, step by step, to help you accomplish your goals.

Bill Good, Author, *Prospecting Your Way to Sales Success and Hot Prospects*

***

Without the organizational data that Arte has so masterfully presented, I would never have been able to accomplish the achievements in my various careers (producer of stage and TV shows, real estate investor, best-selling author of *Nothing Down for Women*, and now my business that presents patented anti-aging solutions).

In *The Natural Laws of Management: The Admin Scale*, Arte has delivered a huge and important body of work by L. Ron Hubbard in a concise and easy-to-absorb format with a style that is engaging and clear. When an interviewer asks me what the key to my multiple successes has been, the truthful answer is that I have applied the amazing technology you now hold in your hands. May you use it well to carve out your own path to your good and noble goals!

Karen Nelson Bell, Best-Selling Author, Producer, Entrepreneur

THE
NATURAL LAWS
OF
MANAGEMENT

THE ADMIN SCALE

BY

ARTE MAREN

BASED IN PART ON THE WORKS OF

L. RON HUBBARD

First Printing 2010
Published in the U.S.A. by Arte Maren, Inc.
1170 NE Cleveland St.
Clearwater, Florida 33755
www.theadminscale.com
www.artemaren.net

WISE IA# 10072901

Publisher's Cataloging-in-Publication

Maren, Arte.
    The Natural Laws of Management: The Admin Scale / by Arte
    Maren ; based in part on the administrative works of L. Ron
    Hubbard.
        p. cm.
    Includes index.
    ISBN-13: 978-0-615-39232-5
    ISBN-10: 0615392326

    1. Management. 2. Organization.
    I. Hubbard, L. Ron (La Fayette Ron), 1911-1986.
    II. Title.

HD31.M37 2009   658

Book design and layout by Maggy Graham, Words & Pictures Press.
Printed in U.S.A.

IMPORTANT NOTE

In reading this book, be very certain you never go past a word you do not fully understand. The only reason a person gives up a study or becomes confused or unable to learn is because he or she has gone past a word that was not understood.

The confusion or inability to grasp or learn comes AFTER a word that the person did not have defined and understood. It may not only be the new and unusual words that you will have to look up. Some commonly used words can often be misdefined and so cause confusion.

This datum about not going past an undefined word is the most important fact in the whole subject of study. Every subject you have taken up and abandoned had its words which you failed to get defined.

Therefore, in studying this book be very, very certain you do not go past a word you do not fully understand. If the material becomes confusing or you can't seem to grasp it, there will be a word just earlier that you have not understood. Don't go any further, but go back to BEFORE you got into trouble, find the misunderstood word and get it defined.[1]

All quotes from L. Ron Hubbard are indented and in bold type.

---

[1] Hubbard, *Science of Survival,* 1951, 2007.

TABLE OF CONTENTS

Acknowledgments

Completing this work of many years' duration, I feel as if anyone with whom I came into contact regarding this book is owed an acknowledgement. We are helped by all with whom we come in contact and then there are those without whom the work would not have been done. Mike Baybak's erudite and experienced editorial advice was of great help in ensuring my language was proper and my concepts clear. Ron Penner kept me on track with his enthusiasm and help. Sharon Maren encouraged my work in many ways and through every rewrite. Cass Warner has my thanks for believing in this book and demanding that it evolve through decades of revisions to a product that can be used by others for the alignment of their businesses and lives. My gratitude to Diana Watson, who offered her valuable experience and expertise—without which this book might still be "a work in progress." The assistance provided to me in the form of administrating the final packaging of this book and all of its aspects was invaluable. In that respect, I would like to acknowledge the help that I received from Tom Zimmerman, Terry Garcia, and especially my editor and designer, Maggy Graham. My heartfelt gratitude to my Muse, Alexandra von Dohmain, who has encouraged and assisted me in bringing this vital tech throughout Europe and who stands as a model for living life as play and reminds me daily that it's all about aesthetics.

My eternal thanks to my friend, L. Ron Hubbard, whose genius and insight provided the motivation and very purpose for this book, for my life's work, and for the improvement of millions of lives across planet Earth.

INTRODUCTION

"It is not man's dreams that fail him," declared L. Ron Hubbard in 1969. "It is the lack of know-how required to bring those dreams into actuality." For that reason, and that reason alone, "Whole nations, to say nothing of commercial firms or societies or groups, have spent decades in floundering turmoil."[1]

The consequences stare back at us as headlines every day: crippling deficits, onerous taxation, failing businesses, and in the prosperous United States alone, more than 30 million people now living below the poverty line. It is not for nothing, then, that Mr. Hubbard further explained, "Man's happiness and the longevity of companies and states apparently depend upon organizational know-how."

If one genuinely understood how individuals best function—their needs, aspirations and the source of their failings—one would naturally understand how groups of individuals best function. Such was the stance from which L. Ron Hubbard addressed the problems of how we cooperate with others—not with administrative gimmicks or authoritarian decrees, but with a uniquely compassionate view of groups as individuals united in a common purpose.

Given what Mr. Hubbard's administrative breakthroughs represent in terms of providing the natural rules by which groups truly function, it was inevitable that his administrative discoveries would become much in demand in general industry and elsewhere. Initially,

---

1 *L. Ron Hubbard: A Profile.*

to meet that demand, Mr. Hubbard authored two books for the working public: *How to Live Though an Executive,* providing advanced principles for increased efficiency, and *The Problems of Work,* offering techniques for such job-related maladies as stress and exhaustion.[2] Like all else that Mr. Hubbard provided in this field, these works represented not a particular interest in business, but a desire to make the fundamental truths of life known to others— and since work occupies so much of our lives, his efforts in the field were appropriate. As word of what is contained in the greater body of Mr. Hubbard's administrative works continued to spread, the Hubbard Colleges of Administration were then founded.

These institutions specifically utilize Mr. Hubbard's discoveries for the expansion of a professional's ability to tackle the challenges of administering and running a group, company or organization. To date, 17 such colleges have been founded in the United States, Australia, Great Britain, Switzerland, Germany, Greece, South Africa, Mexico, Venezuela, Ecuador and Russia. By the early 1990's, some 35,000 individual courses of administration had been delivered to businesspeople from all disciplines: heavy industry, entertainment, communications, health care, and virtually all professional services.

Perhaps of even more current interest is the use of Mr. Hubbard's administrative methods in former Soviet bloc nations where the privatization of industry has necessitated an entirely new organizational philosophy. Russia now boasts four Hubbard Colleges of Administration, with an average of nearly 400 graduates every month. In the throes of the same privatization process, Hungarian administrators have likewise turned to L. Ron Hubbard's organizational policies and established their own Hubbard College. In an

---

2 Books and reference works mentioned in this book including *How to Live Though an Executive* and *The Problems of Work* may be obtained at www.theadminscale.com.

entirely different hemisphere are the 8,500 government employees of Colombia who are currently learning the fundamentals of Mr. Hubbard's administrative methods, just as state and county employees of Texas are engaged in the same.

Recession, inflation, sagging productivity, debts, strikes, unemployment, poverty and want: these all-too-familiar symptoms of economic decline are actually indicators of a much deeper problem— a crippling lack of administrative know-how. If today's businesses and governments could competently apply the basic principles of organization and administration, they would enact workable solutions to what has become economic chaos. Such is the role of L. Ron Hubbard's administrative technology: to provide the means whereby businesses may prosper, governments rule wisely, people may be free of economic duress, and, in short, failed dreams may be revived.

TO BE EFFECTIVE AND SUCCESSFUL, A MANAGER MUST UNDERSTAND AS FULLY AS POSSIBLE THE GOALS AND AIMS OF THE GROUP HE MANAGES. ...

HE MUST BE ABLE TO TOLERATE AND BETTER THE PRACTICAL ATTAINMENTS AND ADVANCES OF WHICH HIS GROUP AND ITS MEMBERS MAY BE CAPABLE. HE MUST STRIVE TO NARROW, ALWAYS, THE EVER-EXISTING GULF BETWEEN THE IDEAL AND THE PRACTICAL.[3]

—L. RON HUBBARD

---

3 *L. Ron Hubbard: A Profile.*

CHAPTER 1

THE ADMINISTRATIVE
SCALE OF IMPORTANCE

Having studied philosopher and educator L. Ron Hubbard's management technology in all of its aspects for over 40 years and having personally worked with him, I found choosing one particular area of his management technology to address was a challenging experience. After all, there are over a dozen volumes of his administrative policy and millions of words written by him on the subject of management. Mr. Hubbard is a prolific author and educator quoted and reported about in books and newspapers all over the world and in magazines from *Forbes* to *Business Week*.[1]

Early in my career, I read a book written by L. Ron Hubbard on executive efficiency entitled *How to Live Though an Executive*. The book piqued my interest and when I researched and reviewed additional management tools that Mr. Hubbard had discovered, I realized his was the first codified system written on the subject of management—and specifically the "Admin(istrative) Scale" or "Scale of Importance."[2]

---

1 Black Dog and Leventhal Publishers, *Thoughts on the Business Life*, a compilation of quotes on business from *Forbes* Magazine.

2 "I have developed a scale for use which gives a sequence (and relative seniority) of subjects relating to organization." Hubbard, Policy Letter of 6 December 1970, Personnel Series 13, *Management Series*.

1

I realized that I had found what I considered to be the basic to all that I had studied on the subject of administration. I then set about gathering what he had written about the Admin Scale and each of its levels or sections.

The "Admin Scale" divides administration into easily confrontable parts. In this respect, it resembles his discovery of the anatomy of understanding as composed of Affinity, Reality and Communication, a triangle referred to as the ARC triangle.[3] While understanding is most sought after in business, relationships and living in general, the mechanics of how to achieve such understanding has never been better provided.

What he did to simplify understanding through his work on the ARC triangle, he has also done with the Admin Scale, through a breakdown of the whole subject of administration into confrontable parts.

The "Admin Scale" is not simply a theory, but a valuable tool for the management of anything.

The Admin Scale is used by executives in small businesses, CEOs of Fortune 500 companies, by artists, homemakers and athletes. In fact, a U.S. government study utilized this tool to plan the water sanitation system of a developing country.[4]

The Admin Scale is vital technology for greater productivity, better coordination and achieving group agreement:

> **I have developed a scale for use which gives a sequence (and relative seniority) of subjects relating to organization.**

---

3 "...the A-R-C triangle—its points being affinity, reality and communication. These are the three elements which combined give understanding." Hubbard, *Modern Management Technology Defined.*

4 "Environmental Sanitation and Integrated Health Delivery Programs," American Public Health Association Monograph Series #4.

GOALS
PURPOSES
POLICY
PLANS
PROGRAMS
PROJECTS
ORDERS
IDEAL SCENES
STATS
VALUABLE FINAL PRODUCTS

This scale is worked up and worked down, UNTIL IT IS (EACH ITEM) IN FULL AGREEMENT WITH THE REMAINING ITEMS. …

The skill with which all these items in any activity are aligned and gotten into action is called MANAGEMENT.

Group members only become upset when one or more of these points are not aligned to the rest and at least some group agreement.

Groups appear slow, inefficient, unhappy, inactive or quarrelsome only when these items are not aligned, made known and coordinated. . . .

This scale and its parts and ability to line them up are one of the most valuable tools of organization.[5]

As in anything in life, if we are able to dissect it, to take it apart and put it back together, we have that much more control and are that much more causative over that area.

The Admin Scale is applicable to your particular job or, if you own the company, to the company. It is also quite applicable to living itself.

---

5 Hubbard, Policy Letter of 6 December 1970, Personnel Series 13, *Management Series.*

Because, as previously indicated, the scale is worked up and down (although it doesn't have to be done this way), I often recommend that building an Admin Scale is best begun at the bottom—starting with a Valuable Final Product and then working each level to the top. The bottom of the scale serves as the foundation of "the building" while goals and purposes are "the penthouse."

The Valuable Final Product (VFP) is exchanged with the consumer for that which you as an employee, the CEO or the company receive as income and profit. What Valuable Final Products are being produced? While the "bottom line" is determined by profit, how the profit is fundamentally obtained is through producing VFP's. Mr. Hubbard describes a VFP as:

> **Something that can be exchanged with other activities in return for support. The support usually adds up to food, clothing, shelter, money, tolerance and cooperation (goodwill).**[6]

As an example: a VFP of an accountant might be "clients whose taxes are complete and filed in a timely fashion."

The next level up from the bottom of the scale is the subject of "STATISTICS," defined as:

> **The independent continuing survey of production or lack of it.**[7]

What statistics should be kept? How are statistics best maintained? How are statistics best evaluated? Understanding the basics of statistics and evaluating production numbers is an extremely valuable management tool.

---

6 Hubbard, "Valuable Final Products," Policy Letter of 25 March 1971, *Organization Executive Course.*

7 "Statistic" (definition), Hubbard, *Modern Management Technology Defined.*

The next level up from statistics on the Scale of Importance is the "IDEAL SCENE," defined as:

> **The state of affairs envisioned by policy or the improvement of even that.**[8]

How would it all look if it were all going very well? Unless you have something to compare to, you're never going to really know how you're doing. The ideal scene helps to create a picture or concept of how it would all look like when it's going well. And thus, when things aren't going so well, one is able to spot what is wrong. You can compare the existing scene to your ideal.

By recognizing where one is and then determining where one could be (realistically speaking) one easily can see the gap. And the distance between the existing scene and the ideal is handled by the next four levels, all related to planning.

"PLANS" are:

> **Short range broad intentions as to the contemplated actions envisaged[9] for the handling of a broad area to remedy it or expand it or to obstruct or impede an opposition to expansion.**[10]

In addition to plans, this entire section of the scale includes "PROGRAMS," which when implemented complete the plans; "PROJECTS," which are used to complete programs; and "ORDERS," which are often necessary to accomplish projects. In this level of the Admin Scale we are dealing with exactly how one accomplishes bringing the existing scene to the "IDEAL SCENE."

---

8 "Ideal Scene" (definition), Hubbard, *Modern Management Technology Defined.*

9 *Envisage:* "to form a mental image picture of; visualize." Scott Foresman, *Thorndike-Barnhart Advanced Dictionary.*

10 "Plan(s)" (definition), Hubbard, *Modern Management Technology Defined.*

Plans are drawn, and programs are written as needed to complete the plans. And there are projects to complete the programs, and orders which make up projects.

Above the Plans section we have the "penthouse" of the scale: "POLICY," "PURPOSES," and "GOALS."

> **POLICY—is therefore a principle by which the conduct of affairs can be guided.**[11]

> **PURPOSE—the survival route chosen by an individual, a species, or a unit of matter or energy in the accomplishment of its goal.**[12]

> **GOAL—a known objective toward which an action is directed with the purpose of achieving that end.**[13]

Are company (or personal) policies aligned with the company (or personal) purposes, headed towards known and achievable company (or personal) goals?

Each level must be in alignment with the other levels. The valuable final product must be consistent with the purposes of the company. The policies must reflect the product. The ideal scene must be in coordination with the statistics, etc.

> **Top is a *goal*, next is a *purpose*, next is a *policy*, then you have a *plan* then you have a *program* then you have a *project* and now you have an *order* then you have an *ideal scene* and then you have a *statistic* and then you have a *valuable final product*. That is the scale of importance.**

---

11 Hubbard, "Policy & Orders," Policy Letter of 25 November 1970, *Organization Executive Course.*

12 "Purpose" (definition), Hubbard, *Technical Dictionary.*

13 "Goal" (definition), Hubbard, *Modern Management Technology Defined.*

Now of course anybody can issue an order if there is a project which is derived from a program which is derived from a plan which is directly derived from policy. Policy is no good unless it is derived from a purpose.

Skip having any plan at all if it doesn't eventually wind up in a valuable final product.[14]

One can rate the effectiveness of a job, a company, a relationship or a life based upon the effectiveness of the scale and overall activity at each level. In fact, the scale defines management itself:

The skill with which all these items in any activity are aligned and gotten into action is called MANAGEMENT.[15]

The use of this scale and L. Ron Hubbard's technical and workable definition of management is a valuable guideline for the evaluation of managers and project efficiency.

Management could be said to be the planning of means to attain goals and their assignation for execution to staff and the proper coordination of activities within the group to attain maximal efficiency with minimal effort to attain determined goals.[16]

The Admin Scale or "Scale of Importance"[17] is a tool with which you can make your job and your life more enjoyable and which permits you to be more effective in them.

---

14 "Scale of Importance" (definition), Hubbard, *Modern Management Technology Defined.*

15 Hubbard, Policy Letter of 6 December 1970, Personnel Series 13, *Management Series.*

16 Hubbard, *How to Live Though an Executive*, page 89.

17 "Scale of Importance" (definition), Hubbard, *Modern Management Technology Defined.*

Here, again, is the Scale of Importance:

GOALS
PURPOSES
POLICY
PLANS
PROGRAMS
PROJECTS
ORDERS
IDEAL SCENES
STATS
VALUABLE FINAL PRODUCTS[18]

My application, utilization and dissemination of this magical tool to thousands of attendees and clients all over the world, in countless Admin Scale seminars I have given, comprise the heart and soul of this book.

---

18 Hubbard, Policy Letter of 6 December 1970, Personnel Series 13, *Management Series*.

Chapter 2

Natural Law

Basic administrative truths exist. We could call such truths "natural laws." If one knows the laws, one has an advantage. The ancient samurai warrior believed that by knowing one thing, you could know many things. The one thing to know is the law.

The underlying fundamental of gravity is the "law" from which other data is being evaluated. It is far more important to be aware of and understand the law of gravity than the speed at which a pencil might fall from a desk to the floor.

If you find that there is a non-optimum business or life situation, then there must be a violation of some law. So what do you do? You look up the law, you review the law and then you apply the correct solution and handle the situation, standardly.

IF ONE KNOWS THE TECH OF HOW TO DO SOMETHING AND CAN DO IT, AND USES IT, HE *CANNOT* BE THE ADVERSE EFFECT OF IT.

This applies in many, many ways and is in fact a key point of life—a fundamental that may underlie all others.

And it applies to you directly on a post and in life.[1]

---

1 Hubbard, "Your Post and Life," Policy Letter of 30 January 1983, *Organization Executive Course.*

This datum has broad application—as does its corollary:

If one is experiencing an adverse effect on a post or in life, then he does not know or has not applied the tech or policy covering it.[2]

If you violate natural law, there are penalties.

Amongst the penalties for violating natural law is effort, lots of effort, with insufficient return. But there is a difference between hard work and effort. Hard work is a vital part in attaining success. But one can work hard at rolling a wheel downhill with lots of mileage for the output or roll it uphill, efforting to move it with little gain for lots of energy put out.

Minimum effort for maximum return is what real management is all about!

If you have areas of your life or business which work only with tremendous effort, there are some violations of natural law, mentioned above. Unless, of course, it has been that way so long that it has taken on the aspect of "normal." "Oh, that part of the business? That's always been difficult." "Oh, that part of my life, nope, that's always been a disaster." Higher-level results are no longer even expected!

There is a standard way of doing things in the scientific or "technical" world. You do a certain action "by the book" and you expect a certain result. However, there seems to be a different attitude in dealing with administration. Rather than a narrow, tried and true path to success, management seems to be considered by many a broad highway of experimentation.

---

2 Hubbard, "Your Post and Life."

In the Hubbard management technology, there is a standard of administration. In an article entitled "Squirrel Admin," Mr. Hubbard wrote:

> When a squirrel is given a circular wheel he will run in it 'round and 'round and 'round. He gets nowhere.
>
> When persons in an organization do not know organizing or their organizing board[3] or hats, they go 'round and 'round and 'round and get nowhere.
>
> There is no valuable production. There is no money.
>
> When you have an organization that has no valuable production, you know that the people there go 'round and 'round and 'round and get nowhere.
>
> They are squirrel administrators.[4]

STANDARD ADMINISTRATION

> There are right ways to handle a group. This is the single fact which most often escapes people attempting to handle groups.
>
> Also, for every correct solution there can be an infinity of wrong solutions.
>
> The right way is a narrow trail but strong. The wrong ways are broad but all lead into a bog.[5]

And there is an excellent definition of "Standard Admin."

---

3 *Organizing Board:* "a board that shows what functions are done in the organization, the order they are done in, and who is responsible for getting them done." Hubbard, *Modern Management Technology Defined.*

4 Hubbard, "Squirrel Admin," Policy Letter of 25 January 1971, *Organization Executive Course.*

5 See note #4 above.

Administration becomes STANDARD when we have the most important points or laws or actions and when we always use these and use them in just the same way.[6]

Standard administration is a collection of truths. An excellent working definition for truth is **"that which works. And that which works most broadly to that which it is applied."**[7] If what you are using is not working, it is relatively untrue. Policies and procedures are the basic truths or guiding principles. Company and personal stability depends upon having such written "laws" available and known to all concerned.

The continuance of an organization and its leaders can be said to be entirely dependent upon the skill, training and integrity of those who handle the administrative lines, details and contacts of the group.

THE BEST GUARANTEE OF STABILITY IS ADMINISTRATIVE SKILL.[8]

As has often been said, why reinvent the wheel? I would rather get into all the creative aspects of living and not spend my time trying to solve things that have already been solved years ago. Do I need to experiment with my "problem" for another three to four months while my income is going down? It would be far better simply to find the natural law that applies to that situation and remedy it.

---

6 Hubbard, "Standard Admin,"Policy Letter of 9 November 1968, *Organization Executive Course.*

7 "Truth" (definition), Hubbard, *Modern Management Technology Defined.*

8 Hubbard, "Stability," Policy Letter of 20 September 1969, *Organization Executive Course.*

CHAPTER 3

SOLUTIONS

We currently live in the Information Age. The first tool of management is information. Any manager needs information—whether managing his/her life, a business, or a small part of a business (the job). In fact, we're all managing something to some degree.

Workable solutions to the problems of business and living are vital for our survival and those of our fellows.

So, how then do we get embroiled in unworkable "solutions"?

ANSWER HUNGER

In my extensive consultations and interviews with managers, it became apparent that some actually considered they were poor managers, born with some kind of "administrative dysfunction." As if the doctor told their parents, "I am sorry, but your child will never be a manager." Nonsense. Management can and should be approached as a science.

There are quite a few things to be said about the subject of management. And one of the things to be said is that there hasn't been a sufficient amount of correct data about it. There are tens of thousands of bankruptcies yearly because of incorrect or ineffective management information. Such information comes about because of man's propensity for having to have an answer, right now, whether or not the "solution" or the "answer" works, and even if the "solution" becomes the next problem. The thinking seems to be that as long as we have a "solution," its actual workability or unintended negative consequences are irrelevant!

In 1969, I was the co-incorporator of Narconon—a highly effective drug rehabilitation program utilizing L. Ron Hubbard's communication and rehabilitation techniques—with its founder, Willy Benitez. I was also Narconon's first Executive Director.

Headquartered in Oklahoma, with the largest training and rehabilitation facility in the world, Narconon is, in fact, the most successful drug rehab program in the world.

In the 1970's, there was lots of noise from the government about how they had "solved" the heroin problem in this country with methadone. This then led to the problem of methadone addicts, who were harder to treat than heroin addicts!

This demand for any solution "right now," regardless of workability, comes about from what L. Ron Hubbard identified as "Answer Hunger":

> **An unfinished cycle of communication generates what might be called "answer hunger." When an individual has, for a very long period of time, consistently waited for answers which did not arrive—any sort of answer, from anywhere, will be pulled in to him, *by him*, as an effort to remedy his scarcity for answers.[1]**

So people try to remedy, as Mr. Hubbard puts it, their "scarcity of answers." They don't have many, so they grab the first one that comes along.

If you had a dimmer switch on a light and you turned down the light just a little bit in an occupied room, that would soon be considered

---

1 Hubbard, "Communication," chapter of *Dianetics 55,* p. 107.

"normal" by the occupants. They could get used to that. If you turned it down just a little more, that would be normal and they would get used to that level of light. After a while they would be sitting around in relative darkness and nobody would make any comment about it. They've all gotten used to what is now called "normal." In his seminal work on logic[2], Mr. Hubbard describes this attitude:

> **Most people have accepted the existing conditions as "inevitable" and toss them off with a "that's life." This is of course an overwhelmed attitude.[3]**

An obviously exaggerated example would be to place a few little pigs in the lobby of a hotel and watch people walk by. A certain percentage of those watching wouldn't even see the pigs. Too uncomfortable. It would make them too anxious. And the others would be milling about, anxiously wondering, "What's this?" And if at the height of their anxiety I said, "It's okay. It's an agricultural convention at the hotel." They'd think, "Oh, okay, agricultural convention." It doesn't really make any sense, but that doesn't matter. I call it "informational junk food." Being hungry, you take the first datum that comes along—and pay the penalty, in the form of effort, as it is usually incorrect and a poor solution.

As the datum is false, and false information blocks effective action, success is always unreachable.

> **False data can cause one to make stupid mistakes. It can even block one from absorbing true data.**

> **One can solve the problems of existence only when he has true data.[4]**

---

2 Hubbard, The Data Series, available as part of the *Management Series* volumes.

3 Hubbard, "Irrationality," Policy Letter of 6 July 1970, *Management Series.*

4 Hubbard, *The Way to Happiness*, Chapter 7, "Seek to Live with The Truth."

When you've heard something falsely rumored about yourself, or information about someone or something that is really distorted, did you ever wonder how that happened? To solve his "answer hunger," someone simply "added" to the "information." In fact, Mr. Hubbard isolated this "answer hunger" phenomenon as the cause of rumor, in The Law of the Omitted Data:

WHERE THERE IS NO DATA AVAILABLE, PEOPLE WILL INVENT IT.[5]

"There's old Joe walking arm in arm with a woman. Who's that woman? Joe must be having an affair." Someone just "puts" the information there, creates it. Then it turns out that the "woman" was his sister.

Now armed with the right attitude, let's take a look at the first section of the Admin Scale, **VFP—Valuable Final Products.**

---

5 Hubbard, "How to Handle Black Propaganda," Policy Letter of 21 November 1972, Public Relations Series 18, *Organization Executive Course.*

CHAPTER 4

VALUABLE FINAL PRODUCTS

Thus, the *valuable* final product of a group must be valuable to another group or individuals in society around it and sufficiently so that it can receive in return things it wants or needs but does not produce. And it must DELIVER its valuable final product, a point most often missed.[1]

The product is what comes out at the other end of your "production machine." It is what your performance is judged on, what your statistic is based upon. It is or should be the vehicle that is getting you where you want to be in life. Ultimately, what you produce determines the exchange you receive.

While goals are vital, it is so much harder (and less efficient) to judge effectiveness by a person's verbalized or even written goals than by what that person actually produces. One doesn't often hear, "Boy, he sure can turn out a good goal." In fact, too often goals are used as a substitute or excuse for production. Something has to come out the end of the conveyor belt of production and it shouldn't be good intentions alone.

Successful people do have very pro-survival goals and purposes. You can see the products of such people around you. But if good intentions actually exist, then they should manifest as valuable final products.

---

1 Hubbard, "Reality of Products," Policy Letter of 1 December 1970, *Management Series.*

It takes effort to produce a product, get it out into the environment and into the hands of the consumer. There are, unfortunately, lots of people who simply lack the motivation or ability to do so. We've all met that kind of person. You say, "How you doing, Bill?" "Oh, great. I'm working on this five million dollar deal," he replies. You meet him a few weeks later and ask, "How's that five million dollar deal?" He says, "What deal?" "The one you told me about a few weeks ago, you know, the big deal!" "Oh, that!" he exclaims. "No, that's six million dollars now. Oh, and by the way, do you have a few dollars for lunch? I'll pay you back when I get my six million."

The Germans have a great name for that kind of situation. They call it *Luftgeschaeft*. Air business. Nothing tangible ever really takes place. (We have a less polite word in English.)

So, before we start having a good time up in the stratosphere of GOALS and PURPOSES at the top of the Admin Scale, we are going to begin with this thing called a product.

Product is defined as:

> **A finished high quality service or article in the hands of the consumer as an exchange for a valuable.**[2]

Why is the product so important? It is what we are delivering, for which we get our exchange. Exchange is a very basic law, a basic truth. **"Truth, by definition—is what is."**[3] Exchange is a law that operates in this physical universe.

SERVING THE PUBLIC

Exchange is a basis of administration and it is inherent in the definition of administration itself. *Administer* means:

---

2 "Product" (definition), Hubbard, *Modern Management Technology Defined.*

3 "Truth" (definition), Hubbard, *Technical Dictionary.*

"to have charge of; direct: manage." It is taken from the Latin *administrare*, to be an aid to: *ad-*, to + *ministrare*, to serve.[4]

An administrator is then, in essence, a minister (one who attends to others' wants and needs). He or she "ministers" to the efficiency and the production of a post or organization. He assists his fellow workers, juniors and staff so that their lot is an easier one, and— most importantly—assists consumers in bringing to them a high-quality, valuable, and finished product. When administration is not dedicated in this fashion we get a self-serving bureaucracy and "squirrel administration." Promoting exchange is what a real executive is all about.

> **Money has to *represent* something because it is not anything in itself but an idea backed by Confidence.**
>
> **It can represent Gold or beans or hours of work or most anything as long as the thing it represents is real.**
>
> **Whatever it represents, the item must be exchangeable.**

Mr. Hubbard further clarifies the importance of exchange:

> **If one is living in a money economy, then bills are solved by having far more than "enough money" and not spending it foolishly. One gets far more than "enough money" by understanding the principles of EXCHANGE and applying them.**
>
> **In another type of economy such as a socialist state, the principles still work.**
>
> **The principles of exchange work continuously. It does not go high and collapse as in speculation or demanding**

---

4 "Administer" (definition), Hubbard, *Modern Management Technology Defined.*

money but failing to deliver. Or delivering and not demanding money.

We see around us examples that seem to violate these principles. But they are nervous and temporary.

What people or governments regard as a valuable service is sometimes incredible and what they will overlook as valuable is also incredible. This is why one has to use surveys—to find out what people want that you can deliver. Unless this is established then you find yourself in an exchange blockage. You can guess, but until you actually find out, you can do very little about it.

Once you discover what people want that you *can* deliver, you can go about increasing the demand or widening it or making it more valuable, using standard public relations, advertising and merchandising techniques.

The fundamental is to realize that EXCHANGE is the basic problem.

Then and only then can one go about solving it.[5]

---

5 Hubbard, "Exchange," Policy Letter of 3 December 1971, *Management Series.*

CHAPTER 5

OUTFLOW/INFLOW

The law of exchange can be an unnerving, difficult thing to work with unless one understands it and uses it to his advantage. The subject of exchange then becomes a simple and powerful tool. It's all about outflows and inflows. You produce (outflow) your product or service for others who want it, so that they will give you what you want (the inflow).

Most "problems" are really problems of exchange. People, all too often, talk about the "inflow" problem that they have: i.e., not enough money, customers, sales, etc. They keep "solving" their inflow problem, but it never solves. Why? It very obviously was never an inflow problem; it was a problem of outflow. You can't solve the wrong problem. Outflow governs inflow.

Outflow, per L. Ron Hubbard,

> **…is holier, more moral, more remunerative and more effective than inflow.**[1]

People stuck on inflow are trying to directly control the inflow. And you can't control the inflow directly—unless you are a criminal. You cannot directly control the exchange unless you are a thief. Thieves don't run the cycle from the creation of product to generating demand for the product to delivery so that they can get

---

1 Hubbard, "Outflow," Policy Letter of 6 July 1959, *Organization Executive Course.*

the exchange. They try to jump over the "invisible wall" between product and exchange. They take the exchange. They try to control the exchange directly, rather than control the exchange through production, through the interchange and exchange of services or articles.

There is no exchange with the criminal or thief. There is only, "You have it, I take it," or "You had it—I've got it now." They can't confront the time and space it takes to produce a product, create demand for it and get it into the hands of the consumer to get their exchange—so they take it now. But the natural laws of exchange are at work. What happens? They get arrested, go to jail, and pay back the time they "borrowed" (the time they couldn't confront).

You cannot directly control the inflow. If you want to see some really tired people, talk to those who try to "handle" the inflow side without the necessary outflow. Show me someone with attention stuck on inflow alone and I'll show you a tired person, losing in the game of life.

The good news is that you can control your production directly (outflow). If you are making ten clocks, you can make twenty clocks. You can get more people to make clocks. You can keep the plant open longer hours and raise the quality. You can do more promotion and do it better.

The simplest and easiest way to get your exchange is to create such a heavy outflow that it simply creates or forces in the exchange. It happens as a natural phenomenon!

If you create a product, if it's valuable (VFP is *Valuable* Final Product), and you get it into the hands of those who want and need it and keep the demand created, you'll get your exchange. That's the law!

An improved balance of outflow to inflow is the secret to reduction of stress. There is no need to keep worrying about inflow or have your attention stuck on inflow. All you need to "worry" about is producing, and if you do that well, exchange must occur. The only way the law of exchange can be subverted is sabotage; someone is throwing the direct mail in the garbage instead of mailing it, or someone is speaking "doom and gloom" in the office, negatively affecting morale. This becomes crystal-clear when you consider that morale is closely connected to productivity and your ability to produce what is actually needed and wanted.

The demonstration of competence is the basic factor of morale, and production is the evidence of competence.[2]

2 "Morale" (definition), Hubbard, *Modern Management Technology Defined.*

CHAPTER 6

THE FOUR CONDITIONS OF EXCHANGE

I t is not simply amount of production alone but, additionally, the quality you must deliver to ensure exchange. L. Ron Hubbard discovered four conditions of exchange.

> **1. First consider a group which takes in money but does not deliver anything in exchange. This is called rip-off. It is the "exchange" condition of robbers, tax men, governments and other criminal elements.**

The first of these conditions is really a criminal condition. *Rip-off* is an attempt to get something and give nothing. And it's the road to ruin.

> **2. Second is the condition of partial exchange. The group takes in orders or money for goods and then delivers part of it or a corrupted version of what was ordered. This is called short-changing or "running into debt" in that more and more is owed, in service or goods, by the group.[1]**

A customer orders five blue pencils to arrive on Wednesday and, two weeks later, receives three orange pencils with a note: "The other two will be coming but they will be green. I hope you don't

---

1 Hubbard, "Exchange, Org Income and Staff Pay," Policy Letter of 10 September 1982, *Organization Executive Course.*

mind." This incomplete exchange causes a backlog and eventual insolvency. And if the pending insolvency is not handled, it can move back down to condition number one: rip-off or fraud.

> **3. The third condition is the exchange known, legally and in business practice, as "fair exchange." One takes in orders and money and delivers exactly what has been ordered. Most successful businesses and activities work on the basis of "fair exchange."[2]**

A customer orders three blue pencils to arrive on Wednesday and he gets three blue pencils on Wednesday. This is legal and fair exchange. It's also what is accepted as "normal." The generally accepted belief is that "if you just give people what they want, then everything will be fine." But, in fact, giving people only what they want does not necessarily bring about expansion. At best, it just keeps your head above water. It does not guarantee survival. The real answer to guarantee success in any endeavor is delivering in abundance. "Normal" exchange does not always bring about success.

> **4. The fourth condition of exchange is not common but could be called exchange in abundance. Here one does not give two for one or free service but gives something more valuable than money was received for. Example: The group has diamonds for sale; an average diamond is ordered; the group delivers a blue-white diamond above average. Also it delivers it promptly and with courtesy.[3]**

Thus we can see that the fourth condition is the only real guarantee of success.

> **The fourth condition is the preferred one. It is the one I try to operate on and have attempted to for ages.**

---

2 Hubbard, "Exchange, Org Income and Staff Pay."

3 See note #2 above.

Produce in abundance and try to give better than expected quality. Deliver and get paid for it, for sure, but deliver better than was ordered and more. Always try to write a *better* story than was expected; always try to deliver a better job than was ordered. Always try to produce—and deliver—a better result than what was hoped for.

This fourth principle above is almost unknown in business or the arts.

Yet it is the key to howling success and expansion.[4]

Condition four is the only one that guarantees survival in abundance and that is achieved by delivering more than is expected. That doesn't mean if somebody ordered ten pencils you send them twenty. That's a good way to go out of business. It does mean that if they ordered ten pencils to be delivered on Wednesday, you send them ten pencils, perhaps on Tuesday, with a few erasers and a little note that says, "Thank you very much for the order."

It is the pluses that guarantee greater survival. And the pluses don't have to cost more time or money. It's a question of care, not cash.

Additionally, how quickly success comes about does not and must not rest on the shoulders of the company executives alone.

Where a group is concerned, there is another factor which determines which of the four above is in practice. It is group *internal* pressure. Where this only comes from executives, it may not get activated. Where it comes from individual group members in the group itself, it becomes assured. The internal demand of one staff member to another is what really determines the condition of the group and establishes which of the four conditions above come into play.

---

4 Hubbard, "Exchange, Org Income and Staff Pay."

Thus the organization collectively, in electing which of the four principles above it is following, establishes its own level of income and longevity and determines its own state of contraction or expansion.

While this is a must in an executive—to establish the principle being followed—the *real* manifestation only occurs from pressure by individual staff members or others within the group.[5]

We can easily see that executive leadership is vital but individual responsibility is also a key factor. It is the group that sets the standard and which of the four conditions is applied or implemented.

It is up to the individual staff member in a group what the group income is and what their own staff pay is. The organization cannot earn more and the individual staff member cannot be paid more than will be established by which principle above they elect to follow.[6]

If you look at every successful business, giving people more than they expect—especially in the area of service—is, in fact, normal. That's the way that it should be. That's the concept that you want to bring into your business or indeed into your life.

You must continuously do those little extras that helped to build up your business.

---

5 Hubbard, "Exchange, Org Income and Staff Pay."

6 See note #5 above.

CHAPTER 7

SUPERLATIVE SERVICE

D o you want word of mouth and customers referring to you? Do you want a stellar reputation? There is a very effective and simple way to do it. *Deliver more than your customers or clients expect and they'll tell everybody else.*

People usually do not talk about "normal," they talk about getting more than they expected. (Of course, they will also talk about getting less than they expected, too.)

I had an interesting experience after having had my car fixed. I got a phone call from the auto repair shop:

"Just wanted to know, how's the car?"

"How's the car? Fine," I replied.

"Well," he said, "we just wanted to check up and see how everything was functioning." And what was my first impulse when I hung up the phone? I had to tell someone else. Telling someone else is a natural response when we get more than we expected.

The Indians of the Northwest of the United States called this act of giving more than expected *potlatch*.[1] Every business or professional

---

1 *Potlatch:* A potlatch is a traditional cultural event held among the native tribes of the Northwestern coast of North America. They are held for the purpose of giving

practice should develop points of potlatch. Many already do in the form of birthday cards and other gifts acknowledging participation with the company. The interesting thing about potlatch is that it escalates. Nowadays if you don't send a birthday card it's probably noticed as missing. So, after everyone's doing it, it becomes "normal" and now we have to take a step further.

Potlatch is synonymous with caring. It is not something that comes "from the head," analytically figuring it out only for the purpose of getting something in return. Potlatch comes from the heart, because you believe in Condition Four exchange as a matter of personal integrity.

SERVICE LEVELS

Current society is weak on service. Have you ever walked into a store to buy something and you felt like you were interrupting them? Ever feel like saying, "Excuse me, I don't mean to disturb you or anything, I just want to buy this. I'll get out of your way immediately. I promise I'll never come back."

Occasionally a real producer will run into a situation where there is pressure to do less! As an example, Andrea works with a group of salespeople and decides that she is going to deliver more than is expected and comes up with a week of extraordinary sales.

The boss says, "Hey, that's good." Then she does it again. She starts doing it every day. Her co-workers are getting irritated. "What are you doing? We're going to have to do that every day." What are they saying? They're saying, "You're making us look bad with this new level of production. We're going to have to work twice as hard!"

---

away large amounts of food and goods. This generosity is then reciprocated at a later date. They are usually marked by lavish feasts, ceremonial dancing and competitions.

PRODUCT QUALITY

In order to constantly achieve Condition Four, we must deliver high quality. A product—to be a product, per the previous definition—must be completed, finished. Further, a product is defined as a **"high quality service or article."**[2] Well, aren't there grades or different qualities of a product? Some products are good quality products and some products are not so good, right? Wrong. Mr. Hubbard says a product is a **"high quality service or article."** If it is not high quality it is not a product. Now that seems very unreasonable but it forces a standard, doesn't it?

Why should there be any lower standard? Surely you should have a high level of pride that considers that anything that comes from you should be of high quality.

If one wants higher quality exchange, if one wants more exchange, then one needs to have higher quality products and more delivery. Such a standard is also the hallmark of a professional. Professionals produce products or services that meet or exceed professional standards. That is what really defines what "professional" means.

There is another factor of exchange, which involves the amount of responsibility you have for any given portion of the definition of a product. **"A finished, high quality service or article in the hands of the consumer"**[3] means the product has to arrive. It has to go somewhere to be exchanged. All too often, someone will produce an excellent product but it never seems to get into the hands of the consumer; there is no real demand for it created via advertising, promotion or other means.

---

2 "Product" (definition), Hubbard, *Modern Management Technology Defined.*

3 See note #2 above.

One must also maintain one's intention on the cycle from creation of the product or service up to the delivery, ensuring that there is adequate and proper exchange.

A positive attitude on sales is important too. Selling has a bad reputation. It's come to mean, in some cases, "forcing something on someone that they don't want and can't afford." That's not selling. Selling has been a major force in the creation of American society. It's been a vital link between the producer and the consumer. And the derivation of the word "sell" comes from old English word *sellen*, which means "to give, deliver." It's the ability to place your product into the hands of the consumer on a rapid basis.

The whole cycle of a product and exchange can be viewed in relation to communication.

> **Communication is the interchange of ideas or objects between two people or terminals.**[4]

In life, one would expect and get an acknowledgement to his communication. In this case, the acknowledgement is not the nod indicating one has been heard, but the exchange of money or goodwill, etc. In fact, communication relates to finance too!

> **If you find finance faltering, you will discover immediately why if you realize that the financial system is a communications system and that communications systems are the background of what you are doing.**[5]

One's intention to accomplish something is a key part of communication: it must be present for exchange to occur. This also means having the courage to push through and overcome the challenges. People who are courageous get things done. They make things happen because they have the courage to make them happen. Of course,

---

4 Hubbard, *Technical Dictionary*.

there are those who like to watch things happen, and there are even those who just wonder what happened!

SHORT-CHANGING YOURSELF

I recall an instance where someone was delivering a product—a great product—and selling it for $250.00. He was not doing well. An analysis was done, and he was told to double his price. Now this person had serious misgivings about this advice, as he felt that he was not doing well even at the lower pricing, so why would he raise his price? "I am starving with the pricing I now have and not getting lots of buyers. I can't possibly double it," he said. And the answer given was, "You are actually creating an imbalanced exchange. You are under-priced." Remember, truth **"is what is."**[6] The product was not worth $250.00; it was worth $500.00. So people were not buying it because they felt (innately) it was worth more.

The lower price made them suspicious. They knew it was a great product, so why was he selling it for $250.00?

What did he do? He priced it in accordance to its true value in the marketplace and he had more buyers than he could handle. Now everybody wanted it. It "felt right" to them.

The solution is not, then—if you are having any problem at all—simply to double your price, but in some specific cases, it might well be good to examine this factor. Beware of this kind of exchange imbalance, shortchanging yourself!

---

5 Hubbard, *Associate Newsletter #4*, 1953.

6 Hubbard, *Technical Dictionary*.

CHAPTER 8

NAMING THE PRODUCT

A valuable final product can be and should be specifically named. The VFP is not something you do. It's the *result* of something you do.

"What is your product for today?" the boss says. "Attend the meeting," is the reply. But "Attend the meeting" is not a VFP. Attendance is a sub product. Motor vehicle traffic school is an excellent example of this point. Students often sleep through the instruction and the accident films shown. And we wonder why traffic fatalities are on the rise? You don't even need to get 100% on your initial motor vehicle exam or for re-licensing!

"Joe, what is your product for today?" "I'm going to call Sam." No, "call Sam" is a doingness. It's not a product.

Here is another example of a sales manager/salesperson dialogue after attending a trade show:

"How did it go?"

"Oh—great. They love us."

But "They love us," is not a VFP and we don't even have any evidence that it's true. Evidence is necessary on a VFP, as a product is also defined as:

> **…a completed cycle of action which then can be represented as having been done.**[1]

---

1 "VFP" (definition), Hubbard, *Modern Management Technology Defined.*

If you really want your product, then the better you name it, the more chance there is that you'll get it. We are naming the product, not for the purpose of having nicer calling cards or a better promotional campaign—we are naming it so that we can eventually get the product!

VAGUENESS: THE ESCAPE HATCH

By not naming the product specifically, you leave an "escape hatch." It is sometimes "comfortable" not to have a clearly defined VFP. It gives you some room for failure—in the event that you don't get the product. If you are set to go out there and get a signed contract, it is very hard to excuse your way out of that. Either you've got the contract, or you don't. "Well, I don't have the contract but they love us!" Well, that is great. "They love us" may be a very good marriage or engagement PRODUCT, but it is not, as we mentioned, the named product. It's just more "Luftgeschaeft."

Mr. Hubbard makes this very clear:

> **IF PRODUCTION IS NOT OCCURRING, THE ABILITY TO NAME THE PRODUCT IS PROBABLY MISSING.[2]**

Note that naming the product requires the ability to do so.

As discussed earlier, the naming of a product is exact and specific.

> **The valuable final products of an organization must be known to, precisely and completely established and defined by top management.[3]**

---

2 Hubbard, "Name Your Product," Policy Letter of 7 August 1976, *Management Series.*

3 Hubbard, "Reality of Products," Policy Letter of 1 December 1970, *Management Series.*

A more effective employee/employer dialogue regarding the trade show would have been:

"Going to the meeting tomorrow, Joe?"

"Yeah."

At this point, the effective manager might sit down and actually confront the desired and/or named products.

"What are you going to get out of this meeting?"

"Oh, I'm going to speak to Sam." (The product is then "people spoken to"—too general.)

"OK, but what we want from this meeting are prospects favorably impressed with our sales presentation resulting in signed contracts." (He could even set a quota of contracts signed.)

"Sheeze, I don't know if I can get contracts," the salesman replies.

Well, what he is really saying is, "I haven't sat down and worked it out, I haven't done my preparation, and I don't feel like confronting the named product."

The effective manager would say, "Okay, fine. I want you to sit down and work it out. Let's figure out how you are going to get the contracts." And they would review the actions and steps needed to end up with the VFP of contracts.

> **The valuable final products of any activity small or large must be very precisely and totally listed and totally continually posted.[4]**

Thus we work out and establish what will need to be done to get the VFP!

---

4 Hubbard, "Reality of Products."

What we want from this particular sales meeting is a VFP or VFPs, which we might name as a "sufficient amount of agreement with our point of view of the quality and value of our product from the people with whom we are dealing (so as to result in signed contracts)." You know that you want contracts as an exchange. The first thing you have to ask is what do we have to do to get signed contracts?

It is always interesting to note what sales people consider their VFP to be. It often gets named as "signed contract." This of course, is fine, but one must take note of the fact that "signed contract," is a reward for the product of "created demand."

Gross Income is really the Valuable FINAL REWARD for which the VFPs are exchanged.[5]

Thus, if "signed contract" is an exchange for our sales valuable, what might the product delivered to the customer by the salesperson actually have been? Well, it surely would have had something to do with agreement or customer understanding of the value of our product (to him) and a high level of trust created that what has been promised to be delivered, will be delivered.

As Hubbard points out:

Failure to deliver is the one point beings do not forgive.[6]

Customer agreement is the key. So we start making a list. "What am I going to need to get them to agree? How can I best get them to agree? Well, let's see, as it's a kitchen remodel, their spouse will have a very important part in the decision, so I'll have them bring their spouse. The color charts—got to have charts." Etc.

---

5 Hubbard, "Product Correction," Policy Letter of 6 April 1972, *Organization Executive Course.*

6 Hubbard, "Group Sanity," Policy Letter of 14 Dec 1970, *Management Series.*

Mr. Hubbard advises that one should first:

> **…establish the product (have), find out what to *do* to achieve it and only then really can you accurately discover what one has to BE to accomplish this.[7]**

One can envision, as an example, that they want to assist society by fighting fires. The first look would be a HAVE: "a society safe from fires." The DO leading to this HAVE is "fires rapidly extinguished when occurring" (commonly referred to as "fire fighting"). The BE is a fireman.

> **An activity has several final products. All of them must be worked out and considered. Then one can work out the sequence of DOs (each with a product) in order to accomplish the final products. Only then can one work out the BE.[8]**

PRODUCT PROMOTION

From my observation, a well-named product tends to promote itself.

An example of its value might be demonstrated at an actor's convention. There are lots of photographers there who are promoting themselves.

"What do you do, Bill?"

"Oh, I'm a photographer."

"Oh, let me have your card. I need pictures all the time."

"Oh, fine."

---

7 Hubbard, "Planning by Product," Policy Letter of 13 November 1970, *Organization Executive Course.*

8 See note #7 above.

But it is likely that he will never call. There are hundreds of photographers available. But now the actor meets our photographer who's just done an Admin Scale on his photographic services.

"What do you do, Bill?"

"Oh, I'm an image consultant."

"What?"

"An image consultant. I find out what image, what communication you want to portray in a photograph and I capture that on film."

"When can we start?" is the actor's immediate response. Why? Because that really communicates as something valuable!

"Oh, it's very expensive." he could add. When it's perceived as valuable enough, the actor will not care! It's never the money. Repeat, it's never the money, as any seasoned veteran salesperson will agree. If a potential buyer or client starts talking about or getting concerned about money, then you probably haven't communicated the value of the product or service. The value is simply not real enough.

Now our photographer can even do a consultation before the photography session, for the same or extra fee, to isolate what the "message" is and be sure he can get his product and a satisfied customer.

Before our photographer's Admin Scale training, his clients used to come in and he'd say,

"Okay. What kind of photograph would you like?"

"Well, I want a picture...you know. I want to look strong."

"Oh, OK. Have a seat there. I'll get some barbells..."

He takes the picture. The client comes back for his photos.

"Here are your pictures."

"Uh. I don't know. That's not me. I don't know."

"Yeah, but you said strong. Look, that's strong. See the barbells?

"That's not what I meant by strong."

"Oh. What did you mean?"

"I don't know. *Strong*."

What occurred was a breakdown of communication. And that breakdown was caused by a breakdown of sufficient early interest on the part of the photographer. The customer said "Strong." What did he mean exactly?

If you don't fully understand something, you've got to ask. If you're really interested, you will ask. You don't know what he means by "strong," so you automatically ask. (Unless, of course, you don't want to appear "stupid." Somebody is talking about something, and you don't quite get it, but you don't want to appear stupid and don't ask them. At that point, you *are* stupid. So try to make it a policy to query what you don't understand. It keeps you smart.)

"What do you mean by strong?" "Well, you know...strong," is the answer.

So he puts a bunch of "strong" type pictures up on the wall. "This is the 'strong' picture set. I'd like you to take a look at this and point out the picture that you like best. Which seems to be the kind of communication or image that you want to portray?"

One cares. One asks because one wants to know.

"All right, well, I like #3, that picture of strength." "Oh, all right. Tell me about it. What do you like about this?" "Well, you know, you see how the head is tilted there to one side? It's strength, but it's a quiet strength. Yeah. It's a quiet strength. That's what I want."

He's got it. He's discovered his image. Now it's simple. No problem. The photographer knows exactly how to set this picture up. He's got some certainty. He has communicated and fully understands what the client wants. No problem. Success is guaranteed. And you don't have to hope; you are certain.

Using this procedure, we organize and promote better. The customer walks in and is handed a sheet to fill out which gives the photographer an idea of what this prospect is really after. Then the photographer shows him five different "messages" in photographs, or maybe ten other actors and actresses in poses that are communicating something. "Which one most closely approximates what you are trying to say?" he would ask, and then—having isolated exactly what was needed and wanted—he would produce it.

The event is the photo session. But all the preparation is done prior to the shoot. By the time he is at work in the studio, he knows exactly what the client wants. He knows how he is going to set it up and how he will shoot it, which is the technical expertise.

The taking of the photograph was the event—but look at the preparation that went into creating that event! That's professionalism.

Back to Basics

If you are having trouble working out naming your PRODUCT, one good method is to cut out all the verbiage, and go strictly down to "What is it that I do?" Then look at the result of that "doingness," and build on that. Let's take a retail picture and frame salesman. The VFP offered is "I sell pictures and I get a lot of satisfied customers." Fine. But "satisfied customers" is something you deliver to your boss, a part of the exchange, isn't it?

"What is it you deliver?"

"Pictures."

"All right, what kind of pictures?"

We are attempting to break it down. We're looking for the truth. If the pictures you sell give the buyers "a special feeling" or "bring them closer to places they may have or would like to visit," that sounds like more of the truth of what you do. And the truth communicates faster and better than anything else.

Someone who is a clothing consultant is an "exterior decorator," as that's what he/she actually does. If he went to a party and introduced himself as an "exterior decorator," people would ask questions; there would be interest. "Well, what I do," he says, "is we sit down and have a consultation to see what you really want to communicate through your clothing. Then I choose the best styles and colors for those kinds of messages or communications. I put that all together in a package and you have your wardrobe."

THE IMPORTANCE OF VALUABLE FINAL PRODUCTS

The importance of the concept and understanding of VFPs to management must not be underestimated. Profits and success revolve around them.

A survey of any activity, requesting a list from each member of the company answering the question, "What are the valuable final products of this company?" can reveal much and can show that many are setting policies and doing things in the company name which have no real relation to what the company is doing and therefore drive the activity in contrary and conflicting directions.

After all, it is the crew, staff members and workers who do the work. When they have to set their own policy and use their own ideas of the valuable final products, you can get a lot of conflicts and upsets which should never exist.

Make no mistake: an activity can be totally unmanageable and become non-viable over just these points. Possibly all labor-management upsets come from them.

1. Policy is set by top management after experience and agreed upon by others. Where policy is needed it should be requested from the top, not set independently by the supervisors or workers.

2. The valuable final products of an activity must be *very* carefully surveyed, established and clearly released at policy level AS POLICY.

Anarchy appears to fail (as it did before the Spanish revolution, 1936) and strong central management succeeds around this one point of policy. Everyone sets his own in an anarchy. Businesses succeed only on that point and the precise establishment of valuable final products.

When the exact valuable final products are known and agreed upon, only then does successful group action become possible.[9]

---

9 Hubbard, "Reality of Products," Policy Letter of 1 December 1970, *Management Series.*

CHAPTER 9

SUB-PRODUCTS

Sub-products[1] are the lesser products that one produces towards the VFP. By knowing and addressing the sub-products which when completed result in valuable final products, one has greater control of the final result. After all, a VFP is a valuable final product. There is a natural sequence, a building of one sub-product upon the next which brings about the VFP.

L. Ron Hubbard developed a set of drills to increase one's awareness of sub-products.

HOW TO COMPILE A SUB-PRODUCT LIST

If you take any VFP and trace it backwards step by step, using a BE-DO-HAVE breakdown of what it took to create it and then wrote up the list as preliminaries, you would have a sub-product list.

Let us take a cup of coffee as the VFP. The minimum sub-products list would divide into what you had to be, what you had to do and what you had to have to wind up with a cup of coffee.

Be: Somebody who wanted a cup of coffee, somebody hatted[2] to make coffee.

---

1 Subproducts: "Those necessary to make up the valuable final products of the organization." *Hubbard, Modern Management Technology Defined.*

2 *Hatted:* fully trained for one's job. "You will notice that various jobs in the society are designated by different hats. From this we get the word hat as a slang term meaning one's specialized duties." Hubbard, *Modern Management Technology Defined.*

Do: Boil water, add coffee, put coffee in a cup, put it someplace where it could be drunk, let it cool until it was drinkable.

Have: Money to buy the necessary, or the ability to make money so you can buy the necessaries or the skill to create the necessaries, water, a pot to boil water in, fuel to make a fire, a fire to put a pot on, time to boil the water, coffee, the skill to make a cup of coffee, a cup to pour it in when made, a place to put it or drink it.[3]

The sub-product checklist can be of great assistance as a guide and as a management tool for correction.

When the orders are issued and VFPs do not appear you will know what you are getting and what you are dealing with: Non-compliance? Sabotage? Overload? No recruitment? No hatting? Misguided staff? or what? Well that would be up to you to investigate and you have a guide of the sub-product list and what didn't or couldn't occur and get busy and do something about it.[4]

An employee, who knows what his or her sub-products are, is far less likely to be distracted by or become involved with activities that are not part of or aligned to their actual VFPs.

UNDERSTANDING

A sub-product list enormously assists an understanding of what an area is supposed to be doing.

It will be found that staffs in a section or department or even division don't really know what it is supposed to be doing.

---

3 Hubbard, "Sub-Products—How to Compile a Sub-Product List," Policy Letter of 24 July 1978, *Organizational Executive Course*.

4 See note #3 above.

By simply taking up the sub-product lists with them point by point, they will suddenly envision the VFP and see what it really is.[5]

PRODUCTION

People can be very busy without producing anything. The busyness of people can sometimes be rather misdirected.

By having an exact list of sub-products a staff gets a very good reality on what productive busyness is. They will coordinate their busyness and drop out non-productive busyness and real Organization VFPs will begin to appear.[6]

And as long as sub-products are produced in quantity and quality, you will always have expansion.

Sub-product lists are made for those who are not dedicated to the cult of poverty and destitution.[7]

---

5 Hubbard, "Sub-Products—How to Compile a Sub-Product List."

6 See note #5 above.

7 See note #5 above.

CHAPTER 10

CERTAINTY

Naming the product creates a certainty, not hope. Hoping has the connotation of being at effect rather than cause. "Gee, I hope I get the job" indicates that the preparation wasn't really done—so it's left up to hope, an absence of certainty.

You have no business hoping and you'll have no business hoping.

> *Hope* of a product has a short term value that permits an activity to be built. But when the hope does not materialize, then any hoped for viability also collapses.[1]

Mr. Hubbard goes on to say:

> The individual section, department, division, organization or country that is not producing something valuable enough to interchange will not be supported for long. It is as simple as that.[2]

> The continuance of an organization and its leaders can be said to be entirely dependent upon the skill, training and integrity of those who handle the administrative lines, details and contacts of the group.[3]

---

1 Hubbard, "Valuable Final Products," Policy Letter of 25 March 1971, *Organization Executive Course.*

2 See note #1 above.

3 Hubbard, "Stability," Policy Letter of 20 September 1969, *Organization Executive Course.*

In the past 25 years, I have observed many a "management system." You may be familiar with the work of Peter Drucker—"management by objectives." I ran across a company that practices what I would call *management by hope*. "Are we going to have a better quarter? Dunno, I hope so!" "Will we get the order? Gee, I hope so!"

And then there is what I call *management by consequence*. Employees do things for fear of what happens if they do not. Now that is a stress environment! Indeed, L. Ron Hubbard equates such an environment with "being serious," the enemy of creativity and motivation. In fact, he defines *serious* as **"when interest is important because of penalty."**[4]

And as I lived in California for 30 years, I would be remiss if I did not share my favorite New Age management system, which I refer to as *management by karma*. "We are going to have a better month because we are nice people and overdue for success. And besides, astrologically this is our time of year."

The winning attitude would be more like "I know the product I'm after. I know exactly how I'm going to get there and I'm going to arrive at my designated destination." And if you haven't done the preparation then you hope that you might get lucky. But the ones who are lucky are the ones who've done their homework.

Of course, as business is a game, it should be fun and treated as a game, as "play with a purpose." Indeed, Hubbard warns:

> **"The more serious you take the game, the less chance there is of winning."**[5]

---

4 "Serious" (definition), Hubbard, *Technical Dictionary*.

5 Hubbard, *Characteristics of Flows,* Philadelphia Doctorate Course Lecture # 26, 9 December 1952.

CHAPTER 11

PREPARATION

Did you ever go bowling and at the moment when you rolled the ball down the lane you knew it was a strike? How did you know? It felt right. The approach was perfect. The approach is preparation and *preparation is a natural law*. You *are* going to put in the prep time, it's just a matter of when: before you deliver (the right sequence) or after (chasing after bounced checks, refunds, fixing it again, re-deliver the right package this time, etc., etc.)

Why is it we often don't have the time to do it right but we always find the time to do it over?

THE SUCCESS OF ANY EVENT IS DIRECTLY PRO-PORTIONAL TO THE TIMELY PREPARATION.[1]

So the law is that the larger percent of effort is in the preparation, the remainder in the actual event. Sometimes people think they can bypass the preparation, that they could somehow skip this part of the "natural law."

Preparation is also the sign of a professional.

If you skip the needed preparation, you will wind up with useless products—also referred to as "overt products."[2]

---

1 Hubbard, "Too Little Too Late," Policy Letter of 28 May 1971, *Organization Executive Course.*

2 *Overt Product:* "a bad one [product] that will not be accepted or cannot be traded or exchanged and has more waste and liability connected with it than it has value." Hubbard, *Modern Management Technology Defined.*

They are called so because they are not in actual fact useful products but something no one wants and are overt[3] acts in themselves—such as inedible biscuits or a "repair" that is just further breakage.[4]

A professional does the preparation, the homework, and then delivers. An unethical businessman or practitioner skips the preparation. He doesn't put in the time, and just doesn't care.

An example of an unprofessional broker might be: A prospect comes into the office of a real estate broker and he says, "I want a $500,000 house." Broker says, "Great. What part of town? How many rooms?" He asks him perhaps five or ten questions. Now he's got a fair idea of what is wanted, but he's really more anxious to get out on the street and find the house. He shows one house after another but somehow none of them are quite right. If the intent is not one of primarily delivering a valuable final product, sometimes—no matter what you show a customer—it's not quite right. "But you said that this is what you want," the real estate salesman replies. "I know I said that, but it is not quite right," he says. And as this scenario continues, the complaining starts: "Boy, is he a pain! Let somebody else have this customer. He changes his mind every ten minutes. I don't care how much business this customer represents, I don't want it." And he just threw away thousands of dollars in commissions. While complaining that the customer didn't know what he wanted, the salesman didn't realize it was *his* job to find out what was really wanted!

It is best to adopt the attitude that there is really no such thing as "bad clients" or "flake customers." There are only managers, prac-

---

3 *Overt:* "we have the word 'overt,' meaning a bad deed." *Overt Acts:* "harmful acts." Hubbard, *Modern Management Technology Defined.*

4 "Overt Product" (definition), Hubbard, *Modern Management Technology Defined.*

titioners, or salespeople who are not interested enough to find out what is needed and wanted. Those who *are* truly interested get the business. The actor we discussed earlier didn't know what his message was either! You do the consultation and he suddenly discovers what he wants to communicate is not just "strength" but "a quiet strength." I wouldn't be a bit surprised if he got up and said, "That was fantastic," pays his money and walks out without his photo.

Let's take a private school as another example. They are involved in the business of teaching. What might the valuable final product of the Director of Promotion be? How about "sending out the promotion." All right, but I can think of an awful lot of ways of "sending out the promo" and, yet, not have a VFP. We could be leaving thousands of copies at the corner drugstore. "Sending it out" is a doingness, and, remember, a VFP should be a result.

How much promo should be sent out? "Well, we got two pieces out this week." That would still be "sending the promo out," wouldn't it? What quality of promo?

This valuable final product of the Promotion Department of the school certainly would have something to do with "communicating what the school has to offer so that it elicits a response." In fact, the promotion probably would have to communicate what the school offers that would be most real to the prospective publics. If your job is to communicate, then it's got to be about those things that are most real to your prospective public. Again, consider the preparation required to get the VFP. The "event" is in the writing and mailing of the promo. Where is the preparation? Well, it's finding out what is real to the school publics. So there is a whole activity that is part of the valuable final product, which has something to do with "a communication based upon prior knowledge of what is real to our particular public (parents of school-age children), which then reaches them and brings about favorable response." And, if we followed this up further and were effective, we would end up with a real VFP of "newly enrolled students" (the final result of our effective promo).

CHAPTER 12

ORGANIZING THROUGH A PRODUCTION CHECKLIST

B y discovering exactly what the final product is, one then can see prior errors in creating the product. Remember our photographer who used to operate on the basis of: customer comes in, says he wants photograph, sit him down, and start shooting? And this was a successful photographer! He was amazed when he realized the number of steps he had omitted in the preparation and the creation of his VFP.

Once we've isolated the VFP, we know exactly what result we want. Then we can also know at that point, with much greater certainty, exactly what steps will have to occur to achieve our VFP. And we work backward from the product, making a list of SUB-PROD-UCTS[1] to get it.

Unless an organization or a person knows exactly what the final product is for the organization or a post, there'll be a lot of busyness but not very much havingness[2] for anyone.

The answer is to figure out the final product and work back through the do of sub-projects and you will then materialize a real organization, a real beingness.[3]

---

1 *Subproducts*: "those necessary to make up the valuable final products of the organization." Hubbard, *Modern Management Technology Defined.*

2 *Havingness*: "The feeling that one owns or possesses." Hubbard, *Technical Dictionary.*

3 Hubbard, "Planning by Product," Policy Letter of 13 November 1970, *Organization Executive Course.*

One would create a flow chart this way.

> **What is the desired product that will also be desired by others? is the first question one asks in organizing. It must be answered before one can adjust or arrange finance or any organizing board.**
>
> **Then one asks what has to be *done* to produce that? And there may be a lot of dones figured out and put in sequence.**[4]

If you're not organizing so as to bring about the valuable final product, what are you organizing for?

You can over-organize, too! Did you ever go into a totally neat office? There's not a thing out of place. And comparing your own desk you think, "I'm a real mess. Look at this. He must be so competent, so effective!" But then you find out he never produces any VFPs. That's his product, "a neat office" or "a well organized area."

He's not confronting. He doesn't have the courage to tackle what's out there. He's got another reason to be shuffling these papers—no real confront to produce VFPs.

I remember visiting a movie executive whose office was immaculate. A place for everything and everything in its place. I was very impressed until I discovered they were going bankrupt—and why? He never did anything but organize. Couldn't confront real live action—getting something done. He was simply always organizing.

REACHING THE RIGHT CONSUMERS

Getting the product into the hands of the consumer would have to include knowing who the potential consumers are so as to create a demand for the product, as well as then being able to get the product into their hands.

---

4 Hubbard, "Planning by Product."

All too often, however, individuals and companies have not done a careful analysis of who their correct publics are and where they can create and expand the demand for their product.

In our consultations with a company or an individual, when we address this "correct publics" factor, we usually find omitted sectors of their public. Because they have always been delivering their product to a particular public, they just follow in that tradition. "Widgets are always sold to young women." Everyone who operates or opens a widget factory does the same thing. One day, somebody thinks it over and says, "Where else can I market this? Whose hands should I put this in? Where can I create more demand for my product?" Suddenly he comes up with a new approach or area and captures a new territory while everybody else is sitting around saying, "Gee! Why didn't I think of that?" They didn't think of it, because they didn't think of it! That's the simplicity of it. They didn't sit down and think about it and say, "Well, where else? Who else? We've always been delivering to these people, now is there any other area where we can create a demand for our product? Maybe if we turn the widget upside down we can sell it to a whole new public."

Finding the right consumer would have to include surveys. What do your customers and clients think is valuable? What do your customers really want? Are these the right customers? Can you satisfy their expectations?

> **What products of the group are economically *valuable*? This is the key point that will be overlooked.**
>
> **What, in short, can this group exchange with other groups or society that will obtain things the group does *not* produce? This is the heart of economics. The law of supply and demand applies.**
>
> **This is too hard-headed an approach for a whole group to decide upon without a great deal of personal work.**

If the group has a past to assess, then it will previously have produced products from time to time that did demonstrate economic value. A search for and a list of these is of primary value.

If the group has no past, it has some experience available from the society which it can employ.

It can be taken as a rule that group members will not identify or phrase the valuable final products. And it can be taken as another rule that it will in the course of time lose those products from its production that were valuable.

Final is another word that will probably escape grasp. Sub-products leading to final products will be given equal billing with the final product.

So three surveys have to be done.

What does the group think its final product should be? This gives willingness and direction.

What have been the previous valuable final product successes of the group? (That did exchange with other groups so the producing group can obtain things it does not produce.) This in a new group would be a survey of what similar groups have produced.

There would then be a period of intense and expert work by or for central policy authority where questions like: Have times changed? Were these items ever thoroughly offered? What was the relative value in light of their cost? Is re-costing necessary due to money value changes? Which ones really brought value back to the group from others? Can we still produce these? Thus a line is drawn up, precisely worded.

Then the final (3rd) survey can occur. This is the issue of the reworked list above to the group to get them to

look at it from their viewpoint and see if it is feasible and any points missed and any expert opinion taken amongst the experts in the group.

The final list of valuable final products could then be drawn and issued as policy.[5]

---

5 Hubbard, "Reality of Products," Policy Letter of 1 December 1970, *Management Series.*

CHAPTER 13

INTEREST

The key to any successful endeavor is being interested.

Interest is a very, very valuable tool. And it is one of the most valuable resources an administrator has. In order to find out what is valuable, you're going to have to be interested. *A professional is interested.*

Frank Sinatra made you feel like he was singing to you. He was interested in the audience. And he got, in return, admiration—applause. They gave him that because of his interest, preparation, and, of course, his talent.

> **A person is interested, and an object is interesting. A person is not interesting. He is interested. And when a person becomes terribly interesting he has lots of problems. That is the chasm that is crossed by all of your celebrities, anybody who is foolish enough to become famous. He crosses over from being interested in life to being interesting, and people who are interesting are really no longer interested in life.[1]**

Many years ago I was interviewed by a magazine reporter in Washington, D.C., with a reputation for being pretty antagonistic in his interviews. Starting off the interview, he said, "Well, Mr. Maren,

---

1 "Interest" (definition), Hubbard, *Technical Dictionary.*

let me ask you a few questions." I answered his questions and then I asked him a few questions. He didn't really want to answer much. "Well, no. I ask the questions," he said. We talked a little more and then I asked him another question. The question I asked was a really interesting one to him regarding how and why he had started his career as a journalist. He started talking. And I asked him a few more questions. Finally we ended off and he got up from his chair and said, "Mr. Maren, this was one of the most fascinating interviews I've ever had. Thank you very much." I hardly talked about me, it was all about him. And he wrote an excellent article.

If anyone is being interesting, they're really saying, "Give me, give me. Give me your admiration, give me attention." But if you are truly interested, then you're observing. You're admiring. You are giving attention, and attention is tremendously coveted.

CREATING YOUR OWN LUCK

Lucky people are people who are really interested in life. They're really interested in their consumers and they start getting lucky. They're in the right place at the right time. Why? They were interested. Opportunities for advancement, for expansion, for wealth, for love, are around us all the time. You don't have to go looking. All you have to do is stop being so interesting and get interested and you'll see them.

Opportunity is always knocking—you just have to be interested enough to listen and have the courage to open the door!

CHAPTER 14

ORGANIZATION AND ATTITUDE

ORGANIZING FOR EXPANSION

There are several major factors to understand as regards expansion: the amount of activity we generate outside of a business which drives in the traffic to the business; the capacity to efficiently handle what's driven in; and lastly, the quality of the product or service that is delivered to the consumer.

All too often, what is driven in simply walks out the back door, meaning that the capacity of the business was not up to handling the traffic. And if so, it must be handled.

Anything which stops or delays the flows of a business or delays or puts a customer or product on WAIT is an enemy of that business.

Good management carefully isolates all stops on its flow lines and eradicates them to increase speed of flows.[1]

A full understanding of VFPs by all those on the "front lines" dealing directly with the buying public is vital. Customers, clients and

---

1 Hubbard, "Speed of Service," Policy Letter of 3 January 1968, *Organization Executive Course.*

patients are aware of when they are actually getting a VFP, whether they can verbalize the VFP or not. A failure to deliver impacts the customer on a personal level also, a point to consider carefully.

> **A staff idling in Reception, offhand handling of callers, wrong address or names misspelled drive off customers. Aside from simply blocking sign ups,[2] these points also REDUCE CUSTOMER STATUS.[3]**

The ability to reach out into the environment and make something occur is vital to expansion. Sometimes, however, to get a company solvent, it's not only necessary to get involved in its marketing, it's necessary to fix the capacity of the business to handle substantial traffic—at which point, magically, it starts getting traffic!

As mentioned earlier, in order to organize anything, it is only necessary to look at the end result and then work backwards from that. At the very start, we can begin with attitude. Some business owners think that they are lucky when a customer walks in the door. If you don't feel that *your customer* is lucky, you had better take another look at your operation. Knowing that you are delivering a product that is extremely valuable exudes a certainty. When that person walks into your business, it is *that person* who is fortunate that you are there to provide a service he or she needs.

One of the best marketing campaigns I've ever run was based on this viewpoint. In the early 1970's, I got a call from the Narconon representative in the state of Washington, and he said, "The state needs drug programs and we might be able to get in if we go there and..." I said, "Call the State Director of Prisons and let him know that I will fly to Washington and do a tour of all their installations.

---

2 *Sign Up:* "Enlist in an organization; also, register or subscribe to something." Answers.com.

3 Hubbard, "The Org Image," Policy Letter of 17 June 1969, *Organization Executive Course.*

If we think that they deserve our program and their facilities are conducive to what we're doing, we will bring it to them." The public relations rep said, "You've got to be joking. I'm not calling them and telling them that." I convinced him to do it and he did. He called back amazed, saying that they gave me an appointment. We went in and I conducted a check of their facilities.

The Seattle newspaper ran an article the next day. It said, "State May Get Drug Program." *If you really feel that you have something of value, that's an attitude that others can perceive.* I truly believed that we produced something valuable—that they were fortunate, not I.

CHAPTER 15

EXPANSION VIA SUB-PRODUCTS

How much expansion in how much time?

In the Hubbard management technology, there is no such thing as over-expansion. If you think that there is such a thing as over-expansion, you'll tend to "solve" it by cutting down your expansion.

> **There is a wrong way and a right way to expand an organization.**
>
> **The wrong way is to add staff and facilities endlessly (like governments tend to do) without adding to the organization itself.**
>
> **If you had huge affluences occurring steadily, you would soon go into collapse if you did not expand also *by organizational units* or branches.**
>
> **In taking over a new field or area of operation, for instance, one errs when he adds that traffic to the basic organization's traffic.[1]**

He concludes:

> **So *over*expansion is only underorganization in the main.**

---

1 Hubbard, "Expansion, Theory of Policy," Policy Letter of 4 December 1966, *Organization Executive Course.*

Mr. Hubbard also provides a summary of workable expansion maxims.

> **In understanding policy one must understand its key and that is expansion. . . .**
>
> **The only ways you can "overexpand" are to fail to expand with new demand and keep pace with it evenly with organizational expansion as well as numbers.**
>
> **It is easier to expand than to "remain level.". . .**
>
> **Organization executives and personnel are overworked only when they cannot afford to expand and thus cannot get the help they need to do the work—quite in addition to there being more problems made by contraction than by expansion. . . .**
>
> **Expansion requires an expansion of all factors involved; and when something expands out of pace with the rest which is not expanding at the same rate, trouble is caused.**
>
> **Uniform expansion of demand, ethics[2] and service into new fields and areas as well as old areas of operation, are needful to trouble-free activities. . . .**
>
> **Any time you do not expand uniformly with all functions, you get an appearance of overexpansion by some functions. The best answer is not to cancel the expanded functions which overreached, but to catch them up by expanding the ones one neglected in support. You will have trouble wherever you cut back an expansion as that is contraction. The answer, within reason, is to**

---

2 *Ethics:* "the study of the general nature of morals. The rules or standards governing the conduct of the members of a profession." Hubbard, *Modern Management Technology Defined.*

advance all else to catch up to the expanded portion while still, more calmly, expanding it.[3]

In this physical universe that we live in, however, things are either expanding or contracting.

It is not very hard to grasp the basic principle underlying all policy letters and organization.

It is an empirical (observed and proven by observation) fact that nothing remains exactly the same forever. This condition is foreign to this universe. Things grow or they lessen. They cannot apparently maintain the same equilibrium or stability.

Thus things either expand or they contract. They do not remain level in this universe. Further, when something seeks to remain level and unchanged, it contracts.

Thus we have three actions and only three. First is expansion, second is the effort to remain level or unchanged and the third is contraction or lessening.

As nothing in this universe can remain exactly the same, then the second action (level) above will become the third action (lessen) if undisturbed or not acted on by an outside force. Thus actions two and three above (level and lessen) are similar in potential and both will lessen.

This leaves expansion as the only positive action which tends to guarantee survival.[4]

As a guarantee to survival, Mr. Hubbard urges:

To survive, then, one must expand as the only safe condition of operation.

---

3 Hubbard, "Expansion, Theory of Policy."

4 See note #3 above.

> **If one remains level, one tends to contract. If one contracts, one's chances of survival diminish.**
>
> **Therefore there is only one chance left and that, for an organization, is expansion.[5]**

There is also the problem of "lazy-easy" expansion:

> **One can of course "overexpand" by attempted servicing in the absence of demand causing, thus, losses in finance. In such a case only concentrate on creating *new* demand, not on servicing old demands. This, by the way, is the most common error in organizations of ours. They shrink because they are not creating *new* demand and concentrate only on creating demand in those already demanding (which is lazy-easy).[6]**

CONTINUED EXPANSION

It always seemed odd to me that when things were not going well or if the stats were going down, everyone wanted to know why; management demanded a reason. But if the stats improved, then what? Nary a word. "Nope, don't want to know. Leave it alone." Now, that really is management by karma! It is even more important to know why something is working well, so that it can be reinforced. What was the cause and what can we do to keep it going?

> **THE CAUSE OF THE AFFLUENCE IS STILL CAPABLE OF CAUSING IT!**
>
> **By reinforcing what caused the Affluence each time, you keep boosting it up to a new higher point until eventually**

---

5 Hubbard, "Expansion, Theory of Policy."

6 See note #5 above.

it peaks at what is truly a stellar range. Now you have a new scene.[7]

In summary, he also lists the causes of organizational failure and the relationship of these causes to VFPs:

Studying back and forth over history, poking about in old ruins, remembering, adding it up, the apparent causes of organizational decay are:

(a) Failure to have an informed, trained top management capable of setting real policy in accordance with the need of the organization.

(b) Failure of top management to set policy.

(c) Company members, supervisors and workers setting their own policy out of agreement with or in ignorance of the needs of the organization and themselves.

(d) Failure of top management to wisely, completely and precisely establish the valuable final products of the activity.

(e) Ignorance of or disagreement with the valuable final products by workers and company members.

In a much more general sense we would have:

A. Unwise or unset policy.

B. Unreal or unstated or undone valuable final products. . . .

The valuable final product list does not come wholly from top management.

---

7 Hubbard, "Vital Data: Power and Affluence Conditions," Policy Letter of 27 August 1982, *Organization Executive Course.*

The list does not come only from the group.

Major social and business catastrophes occur when (a) no list is set (b) top management only sets the list or (c) the group sets the list up.[8]

---

8 Hubbard, "Reality of Product," Policy Letter of 1 December 1970, *Organization Executive Course.*

CHAPTER 16

WANTING THE PRODUCT

E ven after it is "named," how much you want your product is something that must be examined.

Where no real or valuable production is occurring, one has to ask the question, does the person in charge really WANT the product he is demanding? And does the staff member or members he is dealing with WANT the product?

Mr. Hubbard further explores this aspect of "want the product," concluding:

One does not have to be in a passionate, mystic daze about wanting the product. But one shouldn't be moving mountains in the road of a guy trying to carry some lumber to the house site either.

The question of WANT the product has to be included in any examination of reasons why a person or an organization isn't producing.[1]

THE IMPORTANCE OF DEMAND

Now let's add another dimension to our viewpoint on production. How uncompromising are you in your demand for your exchange? The importance of demanding VFPs is indicated in an issue entitled "Financial Management":

---

1 Hubbard, "Want Your Product," Policy Letter of 7 August 1976, *Organization Executive Course.*

The income potential of any usual group is established by the demand for income, not by any other important factor.

In financial supervision on an International basis, this is the only factor one works with. While it is *reasonable* to suppose that income will occur for other reasons and can be achieved in other ways, the actual fact is that only demand by the group produces any income at all.[2]

You are in the "driver's seat." You control your production and your potential income by your demand. "Well, the income was only X this week because, because, because . . . ." No—the income was only X, and that is the cold hard fact.

IT'S ALL ABOUT THE TEAM

Of course, demanding production and income presupposes that you have a team, all of whom want it to grow. And "want" is an active word meaning not just being willing for it to grow, but *wanting* it to grow. Every now and then, in an interview with an employee, he will indicate that if the business got busy, that would be "all right" with him. He could "handle that." But that is a far cry from *wanting* it to grow. Indeed, ensuring you have the right team, each person wanting it to grow, is an important element in ensuring that you get the growth you want with less stress. Every employee is vital to the entire drive towards more success. No one weak link should be tolerated.

No group can sit back and expect its high brass to be the only ones to carry the load. The group is composed of individual group members, not of high brass.

---

2 Hubbard, "Financial Management, Building Fund Account," Policy Letter of 18 January 1965, *Organization Executive Course.*

The survival of a group depends upon the ability of its individual members to control their environment and to insist that the other group members also control theirs.[3]

In tracing a company's failure to grow, I have often found employees who should not have been hired in the first place, or who remained on the payroll long after they were discovered to be far less than optimum employees.

And how did they get hired? Usually there was a lack of hiring protocol—no real hiring procedure, and certainly not one that was based upon successes in the past. And the fact that they are still employed? "Oh, well, you see, I really don't like to fire anyone, it is just a personality thing." Oh, personality? Some of us just love to fire people? We flock to seminars like "Firing can be fun"? No, I don't think so. It is not "a personality thing," but a failure to follow the basics of dismissal.

Most dismissals are difficult because no prior warnings have been given. There has not been sufficient warning, and this makes it so much more difficult to do. If, however, the employee has had a semi-annual evaluation, or has been given several warnings, or has been put on probation—and still is not performing—the dismissal appears to the employee as inevitable. They are, at that point, well aware that their behavior or production has not changed and they are therefore susceptible to being dismissed. Or, as we say in professional management circles, they got themselves fired. (In reality, it's not the company but the employee who fires himself.)

L. Ron Hubbard provides some succinct guidelines governing the hiring and dismissal of employees:

---

3 Hubbard, "Environmental Control," Policy Letter of 30 December 1970, *Organization Executive Course.*

We have then three classes of possible personnel:

1. The willing,

2. The defiant negative,

3. The wholly shiftless.

And he advises:

> Don't confuse a clash of personalities, independence
> and lack of subservience with unwillingness to do. The
> military does this and look at it! If you only want a staff
> that won't talk back, join the army—they punish people
> for communicating or deserting. Some very high-class
> bastards can do some high-class jobs.

> The Unwilling only do or say "can't" no matter what
> solution or task is offered. Usually they don't talk. Some-
> times they are models of meekness. But like a hunting
> dog that won't kill chickens, they are no good to you. If
> they're out of your organization or department, you have
> only the willing left—so why look further in executing
> than being decent. The man who doesn't appreciate it
> isn't with you anyway. So that leaves only one code of
> conduct for an executive to follow, the one outlined here.[4]

Many managers and executives experience upset and added stress
from this one factor alone: employees, quality of. This is especially true for the defiant negative or the wholly shiftless (lazy) as
indicated above:

> His personnel hat excludes the Mr. No and the Miss
> Can't and Master Flop. An executive needs as much

---

4 Hubbard, "A Model Hat for An Executive," Policy Letter of 19 September 1958,
Organization Executive Course.

discipline and anger as he lets the Unwilling in. The first principle of an executive is to accomplish the goals of the organization and department.

And in the case of the willing:

The Willing include the overbearing, the meek, the swift, the slow, the efficient, the worried. Threats and punishing regulations do not help them—only hurt the innocent with the guilty. Tight scheduling, insistence, reason, crispness and ARC[5] help them.[6]

Where you have the willing in your company, it is important to nurture them, to "grow" that willingness even further. Willingness is the personnel "coin" you have to spend.

If you have the "defiant negative," I suggest that you have a little "heart to heart" meeting. Let this employee know that he or she is negative or defiant (the employee will, of course, argue with you). Give him or her a few weeks to change (not the usual 6 months). After all, if you do not see a positive change within days, you do not have an employee who is there to help the company grow, but one who has his own agenda. Dismissal is the only answer.

You must also have the meeting with your l-a-z-y employee if you happen to have one. Let him know that he is lazy and give him some time to change. And if there is no change, dismissal again is the answer.

---

5 *ARC:* "A word from the initial letters of Affinity, Reality, Communication which together equate to Understanding. It is pronounced by stating its letters, A-R-C." Hubbard, *Technical Dictionary.*

6 Hubbard, "A Model Hat for An Executive."

CHAPTER 17

THE "NO OPTION" THEORY

Given that you have a team, all of whom want the activity to grow, there is now the factor of getting it done. And getting it done takes an "unreasonable" attitude, meaning an unwillingness to accept reasons why it did not get done. There are all sorts of "reasons," and they all add up to the fact that the objective simply wasn't achieved. That doesn't mean that you now invalidate yourself or everybody involved or fire them all, it only means that you look at it with the viewpoint of not accepting it. This week, we will do better!

And why is it that we often accept some degree of failure? Sometimes we use certain tools and they don't particularly work. But "the dimmer switch" is at work: the very fact of their not working has become normal. "Oh, that part of my business? Oh no, that never works. It's always been that way." "That part of my life? Oh, that's a mess. That's the way it is." People accept factors of their lives or businesses that just aren't working because it's been that way for so long. It's a perception failure, as the reasons given are incorrect.

We need to sharpen our perception. There are too many things we take for granted. We don't really observe. Why is it that on the East Coast, people drive their cars on parkways and park their cars on driveways? Think about it. Why is it correct to say "a pair of panties" but just one bra?

Here is a perfect example that I heard: someone was riding on a subway train. The person in front of him happened to be sitting on a newspaper. After a few minutes, he asked, "Excuse me. Are you reading that paper?" A moment later, the man stood up, turned the page, sat down again and said, "Yes, as a matter of fact, I am." And the person who asked the question? He just shrugged and walked off—probably thought, "My luck . . . he's reading the paper."

We have fallen into the habit of simply accepting "information" or "data" at face value. We've gotten "flabby" in our perception. We have allowed our perceptions to become dulled and this will affect our production—as human beings and as businesspeople. The way we look at things—our system of observation—is an important management tool. If a manager or an executive is not willing to really examine problems, to really investigate to find the underlying reasons, there will be little success. Indeed, it does take courage to be willing to look closely and observe; observation ability is a high-level management tool.[1]

THE "NO OPTION" THEORY EXPLAINED

A failure to observe and find the real cause allows for the introduction of reasons which are not the real reason. The real reason is always internal and under internal control.

> **. . . [A]n organization's stats are totally under the control of that organization.[2]**

---

1 *Observation* "is not a passive thing. It is an active thing and involves the closest possible study of what one is observing. One should train himself or herself to react in the following manner: if one is in mystery about something one does not puzzle over it, he or she knows at once that if he is puzzled or in mystery or can't work it out, he or she does not have enough data and the thing to do is get more data. The full thought is, puzzle or mystery or can't figure it out—get more data." Hubbard, *Modern Management Technology Defined.*

2 Hubbard, "Control of Statistics," Policy Letter of 28 August 1970, *Organization Executive Course.*

There is a difference between a fact and a reason. The "reason" given for a failure may well be a fact ("the economy was sluggish") but as it is external (and not under internal control) it is not the reason why the statistics are down. When a fact is substituted or given as the reason, when it is simply a factor, it acts as an excuse. And once you put an excuse in place, you don't have to do anything about the situation. The excuse takes the place of action.

It takes courage to be successful. Courage means not having any excuses. Successful people simply don't have any excuses, which are nothing more than options to fail.

Mr. Hubbard goes so far as to say that there is really *no such thing as failure*.

> **Courage could be summed up in, one, being willing to cause something and two, going ahead to achieve the effect one has postulated[3] against any and all odds. There doesn't happen to be any such thing as failure.[4]**

There are all sorts of wild rationalizations that help us fail. "Well, you can't win them all." Why not? Whoever started the rumor "You can't win them all" is now winning them all because everybody else thinks they can't win and so are no longer trying!

"Well, the problem is, it's a slow season. That's why I'm not doing well." That explains it? Summer took five months instead of two? It was a "slow season?" Why is it that during the slow season somebody is always doing well?

At a seminar I gave in Denver, somebody approached me and said, "You know what, Arte, we opened our real estate business in February and we had the best month we ever had. At the end of the year we went to the

---

3 *Postulate*: "That self-determined thought which starts, stops or changes past, present or future efforts." Hubbard, *Technical Dictionary*.

4 Hubbard, Philadelphia Doctorate Course Lecture 42, 1952.

Denver real estate convention and everybody was talking about what a slow month February was. We couldn't figure it out. Then we realized, nobody told us! So, we had a terrific month!"

"You win some, you lose some," is another convenient phrase, as if that explains anything.

Here are some I've actually heard: "My area is different" (salespeople have this as a favorite). "I'll wait until after ____" (insert reason or holiday or any date). "I'll wait until I have ____" (larger quarters, better staff, more money, etc., etc.). "I'm too old or young or fat or thin." "I'd feel guilty if I were very wealthy because there are so many poor people." "It's the economy." "That's life."

"Money is tight!" is another favorite. What does that mean? We did some research. Do you know that there are 43 billion dollars in circulation at any given moment? Where did it go? It suddenly dried up? Somebody's got it.

So there is an important factor here in terms of not permitting excuses. Excuses are simply *options*. Billy goes to jail and then he comes out of jail and then he goes to jail and gets out of jail, and finally we grab him and say, "Are you going to go straight this time?" And he says, "Oh yeah. Yeah. I'm going to go straight—unless I can't make it, and then I'm going to go back to crime." He has an option, and as long as he has an option, he'll use it. That's the trouble with an excuse or an option. If it gets tough enough, he'll fall back on it. And the only reason he keeps going back to jail is because he's got this option!

In one of my seminars, I had one woman tell me that, in her family, passed down from generation to generation, was the "fact" that no one in the Johnson family ever had any money. It was like a financial genetic affliction, an economic disaster that befell the Johnson family.

She soon realized that that was ridiculous. It was just an idea. She could change her mind. She's probably gone on to great wealth, much to the chagrin of the family. "Did you hear that she has money?" "Oh no! It's terrible." And why? Because she would have set a new, higher standard.

There are also various styles of excuses. A subtler one is to use comparisons, such as, "Well, I'm not too healthy, but I'm a lot healthier than that wino in the gutter." That would be an interesting rationalization. "Well, my business is not too good, but we're not bankrupt." "The marriage is not going too well, but we're not divorced." Great, but you didn't get married to be "not divorced." That wasn't the purpose!

How about "Most small businesses fail within the first year."

I had a person tell me when he got his new franchise that he was told, "Bill, it's going to take you two years to make a profit." How long do you think it took him? About two years! Could you imagine if we removed that option? "Bill, here is your certificate. Now, if you don't start turning a profit in one year, we're going to pull this certificate." He would have made a profit in one year.

If you tell a person to get something done in five hours, how long do you think they will take?

Excuses are a primary form of false information. It takes courage to create and deliver a product—a real product—into the hands of a consumer, and get an equitable return.

It takes courage to be unreasonable. The physical universe itself is unreasonable. You can't bargain with the physical universe. The physical universe just won't listen. It runs very tight control, called time. Every second ticks by relentlessly. You can't request, "Could you hold up those seconds a minute and give me about 10 minutes more?" It's very "unreasonable." You want more time? Tough. Can't have it. "Aw, if I just had five more minutes..." Too bad. Doesn't matter what your reason is, you can't have more time. Life just goes on one second after the next, relentlessly. It's unreasonable.

One sure way to combat the excuse "disease" is to avoid "reasonableness" and adopt L. Ron Hubbard's definition, as it underscores a further natural law of management (and life!):

> **An objective can always be achieved. Most usually, when it is not being achieved, the person is finding counterintention in the environment which coincides with his own (this is reasonableness), and his attention becomes directed to his own counter-intention rather than to his objective, i.e. he has interiorized into the situation.**[5]

Notice the use of the word "always." It doesn't say an objective can sometimes be achieved "if it's not snowing" or "except during summer" or "except when I don't feel well." Notice also the word "finding." This means actively looking for; it's not a passive word. It's not, "Well, I was standing around, and along came this counter-intention." No, it's *finding* counter intention.

A salesperson has a quota of twenty sales for the week. Rather than work out exactly how the sales would be made, the salesperson doesn't believe that it can be done, or in some way has some "back-off" on reaching the quota. This opens the door for the salesperson to *find* counter-intention (distractions and other challenges) that "prove" that the target cannot be reached. But, in fact, it was simply reasonableness.

You are not going to be successful in life or business if you provide options for failure. If you go into agreement with another person's "option" to fail, it's actually an invalidation of his or her real potential, too!

---

5 "Reasonableness" (definition), Hubbard, *Modern Management Technology Defined.*

We give ourselves the failure option as an excuse for not making it go right. And we now play the game of life with this "option" called failure. "Yes," you say, "but you can't be successful all the time!" The guy who said, "You can't be successful all the time," is a guy who needed some agreement for his failure. He wanted company. He spread the rumor.

Being unreasonable is what the physical universe is doing and therefore when you parallel it, when you act *as if* you are cause, you keep the higher standard; you start winning. It takes more courage to be unreasonable.

Aristotle said courage is so important that it is the first of human qualities, which guarantees the others.

An "unreasonable" person would name products exactly And the products intended would arrive. Indeed, being unreasonable, you would totally *expect* them to arrive. Mr. Hubbard refers to this as a **positive postulate**.[6] There's simply no consideration that what you expect to happen might not happen. It is totally positive.

In fact, if you communicate any reservation to those with whom you work, they will perceive your less than full intention. Now there is room for less than full compliance. But if you don't have any reservation, boy, that spreads around. It's the reverse of the "dis–ease." "Oh, Joe said we have to have it by three. He really means it." And suddenly they move heaven and earth to get it there at three o'clock.

It is very gratifying to see what people are actually capable of doing when you start becoming more unreasonable with them. *Being*

---

6 *Positive Postulates:* "It's not only that there is no negative given attention to but it does not assume that any negative is possible. It doesn't pay any attention to negatives. . . . Your determination or intention . . . is of course a positive postulate. It will be ineffective to the degree that you doubt it." Hubbard, *Modern Management Technology Defined.*

unreasonable is really an admiration of that person. You are saying, "You are capable of more."

"Gee. I can't do that," someone says. What a terrible response it would be to say, or think, "Yes, well, I guess you can't." And it is highly effective to become more unreasonable about your own potentials and your own capabilities. Now, "unreasonable" does not mean "nasty." Unfortunately, managers or administrators in general sometimes mistake being unreasonable with being angry or nasty. "You'd better have it on my desk by seven." No, that's already implying that you have some suspicion that it's not going to get there. That's already an "option."

A very strong conviction can be delivered quite cheerfully, but people know you mean business. You can tell children 7 p.m. is bedtime, but if you don't really mean that 100%, they know it, and at 8 p.m. they're still up.

The idea of not giving them an option places confidence in the person to whom you're communicating. It's as if you are saying, "I know that you're going to deliver the furniture on time." And when they start explaining to you how they can't, you can handle it with validation, not anger:

"Yeah, but if we get a flat tire, or..."

"No, no, no, no, Joe. You're not following me. It's going to be there at 4:00. That's your job and I expect it to be there at 4:00. I don't expect you to get any flat tires."

"Yeah, but what if... what if..."

"No, no, no, no... No 'what-ifs.' A to B. You will be there at four."

That's the game you want to play. You're generating confidence. And your confidence communicates to others. Thus, if you parallel that same physical universe unreasonable attitude, you will be in harmony with it. Watch how lucky you get!

THE "NO OPTION" STANDARD

If you set a demanding standard, you'll get results. If you leave a lot of room for failure, that's what you'll get.

As mentioned earlier, in my work with Narconon, I've spoken to lots of people who have been constantly in and out of jails. They have given themselves an "option." They haven't realized that it is only because they have such an "option" that they wind up in jail again! They don't realize that people who do not return to jail have not given themselves the option of "going straight unless I can't make it."

If a person wants to go from A to B he has to have a real intention to do so. He's going to move from A to B. If he has an "option"—if he has a slight variation on that intention, like "maybe I will"—if it's a bit vague—he has to that degree, a counter-intention.

If the attitude is, "I'm going to go from A to B as long as I don't have too much trouble," he has options. One, of course, has power of choice. One can always change one's mind—if it is done causatively, and not at the effect of the environment.

Lacking discipline, you'll end up spending your time looking for the ways out of going from A to B instead of the way to arrive at B. The trouble with any option is, when do you take the option? The guy says, "I'm going to go straight unless I can't make it." When does he exercise the option? A new job or success could be right around the corner!

My good friend Dionisio fought in the Cuban revolution. On December 31st, 1958, at about 8 p.m., he literally gave up. He had been in the mountains for two years, hadn't seen his family and he was living under terrible conditions. He decided to give it up. He started walking down the mountain. It would have meant sure imprisonment or death. His friends saw him, grabbed him, knocked him unconscious, and dragged him back up the mountain. Four hours later, Batista, the dictator of Cuba, fled the country and the revolution was over.

When do you exercise the option?

I remember one vice president who was very proud about all of the overtime that employees put in because it showed that the staff was really "with it." They were willing to stay there late. But the reason they would stay late was because they had all that overtime! As long as they had the option, "Well, I'll do it tonight. I've got time, I'll just do it tonight," they wasted a lot of time during the day.

We removed the option. "There's no more overtime. We will pay bonuses for production and cut out overtime." Suddenly, nobody stayed over and production increased!

An individual who intends to go from A to B, but encounters some "interference" (which he can't confront) and decides to go to C instead, is in trouble. C has its problems too. So he decides to go to D, and D has its problems, so he decides to go to E. Each time, the intention is watered down and the game gets smaller and smaller.

Every time you back off or flinch, the game gets smaller and smaller and smaller. You finally get to the point that you are playing a tiny game, and boy, are there problems! You'll have more problems in a little game than going from A to B in the first place.

This concept works in business and in life as well. There you are doing well and intending to get to your chosen point B. Suddenly along comes Sam and he offers you a new job in Gizanzibar.

You say, "Well, I was going to plan my work and work my plan, but then Sam came along and he told me about Gizanzibar and I thought it would be better." That's simply not moving from A to B. That is finding ways *not* to go from A to B.

Now perhaps that sounds silly. Why would you decide to go from A to B and then spend all that time looking for ways not to go from A to B? That's what makes it a sickness; that's what makes failure a disease. It's really a failure to confront. In such failures, the solution becomes the next problem. A good solution is one that doesn't become the next problem.

Let's take an example from our furniture company. We know we're supposed to get the furniture from A to B but it arrives late. We say to the driver, "Why is it late?" He says, "Oh. Flat tire. We had a flat tire." "Oh," you say. "Flat tire." And you tell your customer, "It's late because he had a flat tire." And the customer says, "Oh. A flat tire." And he tells his boss, etc. Now everybody is getting the disease. Your truck driver got the disease and he gave it to you. "Flat tire." You got it and you passed it on. Contagious.

Your truck driver knew that you would not accept, "I stopped off for half an hour." You're not that "reasonable." So what happened? He got a flat tire. Did he knowingly sit down in the car and "will" the flat tire? No, not necessarily, but it happened!

The better way to deal with this example would have been: "A flat tire?"—you respond incredulously. "Twenty thousand square feet of highway and you found the nail!" In other words, it's not as if he went looking for the nail. It is simply that people will find or seek out your level of reasonableness. He knew you wouldn't accept, "I stopped off." So, somehow, unconsciously, "magically," he got a flat.

What do we do with this company having lots of trouble with flat tires? I'm asked to come into the company, at great expense, to solve this incredible problem. They're just having one flat after the next.

Of course, they're giving all sorts of "reasons"—being "reasonable" as to why all these flat tires. "Well, you know they don't make tires like they used to." "There are a lot of nails out there these days." "People are careless."

What do I do? I assemble all employees to issue an order in the name of the president of the company. Very cordially, I say, "I have something I'd like to tell you. Flat tires are hereby prohibited. No longer allowed. That's all. Thank you very much." And the truck drivers all walk away saying, "What is he talking about? Is he crazy? No flat tires, ridiculous."

But what happens? Suddenly, as if by magic, the flat tire graph goes down. People are not getting flats as much any more. Why? Because they are prohibited. They don't have the flat tire option. I've taken it away. It doesn't exist.

Next week the flat tire graph falls even further. Almost no flat tires. Why? We simply removed the option.

What you permit will occur. You set the standard. What you allow in your space you will have. What you are reasonable enough to accept you'll get. If you accept "flat tires" in your life or business you'll get them. But if you decide, "Wait a minute, I'm not going to have any flat tires—I don't agree with that any more," suddenly you'll have less and less flat tires. Pretty soon a "flat tire" wouldn't think of becoming involved with you. That's a very unreasonable attitude.

The areas that you are very reasonable about will always be wrapping themselves around your neck. You don't want to deal with failure? Fine. Get rid of the option. You no longer have the option. You're no longer reasonable. You will soon discover that being unreasonable is fun.

Any person is capable of being successful and can be put at a cause position. You don't have to be nasty about it, either. Removing the "option" to have flat tires was not done angrily—it was friendly but firm. Being unreasonable also shows how much you care.

Rules can help guard against options. Many people have personal rules. "I will never borrow." And they're more successful. The rule guards against the "option."

There's always a point in an option environment where you can fall back; there is always that "option." In March of 1519, General Hernando Cortes of Spain, on a mission to conquer Mexico, burned his eleven ships as soon as they landed, committing himself and his forces to their mission of conquering Mexico. He removed any option—they had no choice but to be victorious—and they were!

You could say that options are a form of negative thinking. The trouble with negative thinking is that it is usually a self-fulfilling prophecy. Human beings like being right, and, being quite capable of making anything happen that they postulate, they will ensure the negative occurs—so they are right!

And there is the classic story of the elderly gentleman who had a roadside frankfurter stand. He did quite well. He promoted, had big signs, bought high-quality meat, gave great service, advertised locally, etc. Then his son came home from Harvard—economics major that he was—and "explained" to his dad how "times were tough." He urged his dad to cut down on expenses to conserve, and he should listen to him as he had an MBA and a Ph.D. (everything but a J-O-B!). Dad figured he paid quite a bit for this sage advice (he paid his son's entire college education from his stand's profits) and he ought to listen, so he cut back on the promotion. He reduced his advertising, he cut the quality of his franks, and what do you know? He discovered his son was right—times were tough!

If you have no options, if they don't exist for you, you'll tend to be more positive and more effective. Remember the "positive postulate"?

It's not only that there is no negative given attention to but it does not assume that any negative is possible.[7]

---

7 "Positive Postulate" (definition), Hubbard, *Technical Dictionary*.

You may recall the best-selling book *Jonathan Livingston Seagull*. The book celebrated man's unlimited potential. What most people don't know is that Richard Bach had been turned down by nineteen publishers before the book was finally published and became a bestseller! R.H. Macy tried and failed seven times before Macy's department stores became a household word.

Doubting just makes it easier to fail. It's more comfortable and gives you something to lean on. The fact is, you can make it go right if you have enough courage!

All too often we wait for the external environment to change before we change: "after the fall (or winter, or summer, or the holidays)"—"when the kids are in (or out of) school"—"next weekend." Waiting is simply another form of failure—of lack of courage. Waiting is the effect of things.

Suppose you didn't have failure as an option? Supposing you just removed failure from your whole conceptual "kit bag." It doesn't exist. That only leaves making it go right all the time. It takes courage to be successful.

And, if you agree and decide that failure is not possible, and then fail, do you now feel bad and invalidate yourself? Do you decide that it is a concept only for others? No! Acknowledge it. Know that you had something incorrect. Fix it, and then make it go right. If it didn't go right, you don't then conclude that there must be something wrong with your ability to postulate. That would be invalidation.

It's simple. Maybe that is why it is so hard to grasp. For our delivery example, you know that the packages can and will get delivered on time—that is all. And if you communicate that, and your intention is there, they get there on time. And you know why they get there on time? Because you intended it!

And with such intention, if the delivery still doesn't arrive on time, then you may well be getting active counter-intention. And if you accept "reasons," then it may well be that you didn't really want or care enough to get it delivered on time either!

CO-MOTION WITH THE PHYSICAL UNIVERSE

It is a question of being in harmony with the laws of the physical universe. Naming a product is a tool of management. You are senior to any tool. You are the person who's going to make this thing work one way or the other. And that takes being unreasonable, which is a very professional viewpoint.

The next time you hear somebody making excuses, know that they have a social disease called failure. They caught it from someone else. Listen to others being reasonable. No more options. Catch yourself when you start coming up with your own little options. You get into the car and you're late and you say to yourself, "I'm always late." Well, you will certainly keep being late if that's what you think!

CHAPTER 18

PROBLEMS

Individuals producing a product often will encounter barriers and problems. Problems are not something to be avoided; they are really something to be welcomed. If we are going to play a game, which we're certainly doing in business and life, we're trying to move from A to B. Obviously, as a game, it's going to have opposition. What we might call problems are really challenges or opportunities. Why get uptight about it? If you are going to play a game, there is going to be opposition. Can you imagine if you are playing football, somebody tackles you and you say, "Get off of me! What are you doing?"

You can be "reasonable" about your problems too. If you've had a difficulty or a problem for quite some time, and it's not solving, I can promise you that it's not the problem. You cannot solve the wrong problem. I have never found anybody who didn't have terrific solutions. It's not solutions you need; *it's the perception necessary to locate the actual problem so that you are not dealing only with symptoms*. In fact, the most sane reaction is to "own the problems" rather than being detached from them as a spectator (someone who is never really involved, so they can't get close enough to inspect the real reason).

It's been said that if we all took our problems, put them all on the table, and left the room—and you could come back and choose any set of problems you wanted—which ones do you think you'd choose? Your own! That's right. You're used to them. They're yours.

Some people are in love with their problems! Did you ever have somebody tell you a very complex problem, this complex thing that had absolutely "no solution"? Perhaps you listened and you listened and at the end you said, "Oh, I'll tell you what you can do about that. That's simple. Just do this." What do they say? "Naw, naw. That won't work. I tried that." "No, it *will* work," you say, "It'll work. It's easy. You can't see it 'cause you're in it. I'm telling you..." And if you persist they get uptight and say, "You don't understand my problem." (This thing that they've worked so hard to put together that had no solution!)

And what if you had no problems at all? None! Everything that you attempted to do, you did. You had no opposition. You'd probably invent problems just to have some kind of game! Show me a person who has a lot of "unsolvable" problems and I'll show you someone who doesn't have enough problems. They have such a scarcity of problems that they are making a meal out of the ones that they have for fear that if they lost this problem they wouldn't have any more.

> **A person begins to suffer from problems when he does not have enough of them. There is the old saw (maxim) that if you want a thing done give it to a busy man to do. Similarly, if you want a happy associate make sure that he is a man who can have lots of problems.**[1]

The next time somebody gives you all their problems, don't give them an easy solution because that takes the game away. What you've got to do is when they've finished this long dissertation, this complex problem, you say, "That is the worst thing I've ever heard. How are you possibly going to handle that?" They'll probably say, "No, wait a minute. That's not so difficult. I can handle that."

---

1 Hubbard, "The Reason Why," Bulletin No. 84, 15 May 1956.

Solving problems entails locating the causes. Locating the causes entails observation. Unfortunately, observation is becoming a lost art.

Spectatorism is very great in our modern society.

Because some people cannot conceive of *causing* anything, they just watch it. They don't *do* anything. They are not PARTICIPANTS. They are spectators.

You see this in magazines. Hee hee hee articles about how *odd* this is or that is. No understanding of it. It's just odd and one watches it in a detached sort of way.

Below this is somebody who doesn't even notice. Such a person has to come up scale just to be a spectator.

And, Mr. Hubbard concludes:

What we need are more PARTICIPANTS, more team-mates.[2]

SUMMARY

A product has to be tangible and something that is needed and wanted (making it valuable). And it must be something that can be delivered. Based on natural law, if you want to increase your inflow, it is only necessary to increase the quantity and quality of your outflow and all good things will come. Name exactly what it is that is wanted and organize in order to get it. Avoid rationalizing. And know that it is possible to be unreasonable and enjoy it!

Validate yourself and others by not accepting any less than what you know you, or they, are capable of being, doing or having.

---

2 Hubbard, "Spectatorism," Policy Letter of 14 January 1969, *Organization Executive Course*.

CHAPTER 19

MANAGEMENT BY STATISTICS

Being unreasonable and having no options increases production. And production is regulated and monitored by statistics, the next level up on the Admin Scale.

Stats are best represented on graphs. *A graph helps keep you unreasonable.* The graph does not tell you that "it snowed" and therefore "things were difficult that day." It doesn't give you any "reasons." It simply shows production or non-production. Products are a physical reality, and if you wish to manage with reality, you must have real information. Management survives to the degree that it has sufficient data to determine what is working so as to reinforce it—and what is not functioning well, so as to change that action or system. And the first type of information needed is not lengthy reports, but correct, condensed data: a stat. A stat is:

> **The only sound measure of any production or any job or any activity.**[1]

It's a sound measure because it's devoid of opinion. There's no opinion in "the number of _____." There are either so many or so few.

Statistics are defined as:

> **A number or amount compared to an earlier number or amount of the same thing. Statistics refer to the quantity of work done or the value of it in money.**

---

1 "Statistic" (definition), Hubbard, *Modern Management Technology Defined.*

The independent continuing survey of production or lack of it.[2]

Accurate information is oxygen for management. Statistics provide an efficient glimpse at company productivity and condition. And you're better off having statistical data sooner rather than later.

THE EARLY WARNING SYSTEM

If the stat is down, something is wrong. Graphs show this by visual means. There is a reason for a stat dropping. It's not "karma" or some "natural phenomenon." Some people attempt to excuse a down stat by inventing "reasons," a huge error.

> **The one big god-awful mistake an executive can make in reading and managing by graph is *being reasonable* about graphs. This is called JUSTIFYING A STATISTIC. This is the single biggest error in graph interpretation by executives and the one thing that will clobber an organization. . . .**

> **Never JUSTIFY why a graph continues to be down and never be reasonable about it. A down graph is simply a down graph and somebody is goofing. The only *explanation* that is valid at all is, "What was changed just before it fell? Good. Unchange it fast!" If a graph is down it can and *must* go up. How it is going to go up is the only interest. "What did we do each time the last few times just before it went up? Good. Do it!"**

> **Justifying a graph is saying, "Well, graphs are always down in December due to Christmas." That doesn't get it up or really even say why it's down!**

> **And don't think you know why a graph is up or down without thorough investigation. If it doesn't stay up or**

---

2 "Statistic" (definition), Hubbard, *Modern Management Technology Defined.*

continues down then one didn't know. It takes very close study on the ground where the work is done to find why a graph suddenly rose or why it fell.[3]

Keeping and maintaining statistics is a matter of confront. What makes graphs so useful for those who want to play the game successfully is the fact that they represent actuality. We don't want to invalidate the overall production because of a down week after many up weeks, but we don't want to allow the "option" for lower stats to go by unacknowledged either.

If we permit a down week—because the week before was so high—we are being reasonable and validating a down stat, which will bring more down stats. The reverse is true as well. When a stat has been in the low range of the graph and then goes slightly up, it should be validated, even when only a slight rise.

> **Also, it's a bit mean to nag around about a rise. "But it isn't much of a rise, you're really in too low a range to have a rise count . . ."**
>
> **A rise is a rise. They at least got more. Now, better organizing, they will get more than that. Week by week it goes up.**
>
> **Similarly to discount a fall just because stats are high high high is folly. They *could* do week before last's as they did it. So what was wrong that they couldn't do it again? If they got exhausted at it week before last they need more help, obviously. Or better organization.[4]**

And it was not just the down stat not confronted! The problem with this particular graph occurred not only at the low point, but at the

---

3 Hubbard, "Statistic Interpretative, Statistic Analysis," Policy Letter of 6 November 1966, *Organization Executive Course.*

4 Hubbard, "Reading Statistics," Policy Letter of 5 May 1971, *Organization Executive Course.*

high point! What wasn't confronted, what wasn't handled, was not just the low week, but also in the high week!

INVESTIGATING UP STATISTICS

Something very effective was occurring through the upswing but nobody found out what it was! Then something changed and the stat crashed out the bottom. Why is it that when things aren't going well everyone wants to know why? The lower it goes, the more agitated they can get.

But what happens when a stat goes up? If the statistic is rising, everyone relaxes. And what happens? The statistic drops because nobody found out why it was going up in the first place! And when it drops, what do they say? "Well, of course it dropped. It was up so high." Which is, naturally, totally "reasonable." In other words, it was expected to fall, and of course it fell.

An inspection and investigation of an up statistic should be at least as interesting, if not more so, than the down stat. After all, it's positive! The time to investigate is on the upswing when it's going well. That's a lot more fun, and it's a vital action. It's hardly ever done to the degree that it should be. When things are going well, you want to find out why. And when they're not going well, you're going to find out why also.

Statistics rise or fall because of positive or negative changes. Statistics are a matter of changes. Some kind of positive change in some operating procedure was introduced near the point that started things going on the climb. If a stat drops, something changed. Whatever positive factor was put in was taken out or altered.

When statistics change radically for better or for worse look for the last major alteration or broad general action just before it and it is usually the reason.

Example: Letter out statistic falls and falls. In investigating, look for the last major change in that area and if possible cancel it and the statistic will then rise.

Mr. Hubbard further explains, in the same issue, how he arrived at this management concept:

I learned this while researching the life force of plants. Every time I saw a research bed of plants worsen, I queried what routine had been varied and found invariably some big change had been made that wasn't usual.

It is change that changes things for better or for worse. That's the simplicity of the natural law.

If you want to hold a constant condition, don't change anything.

If you are trying to improve something make changes cautiously and keep a record of what is changed. Then you watch statistics and if they decline you hastily wipe out the last change. And if they improve you reinforce the change that began it.[5]

Of equal importance to changes are comparisons. Comparison is as vital in stats as it is in evaluating anything.

Statistics must be studied and judged alongside the other related statistics.

A rising income graph can even be shown sometimes as an actual threat to an organization if the *delivery* stats

---

5 Hubbard, "Statistics, Actions To Take, Statistic Changes," Policy Letter of 1 February 1966, *Organization Executive Course.*

are down and stay down. It means the organization is selling and not delivering and may very well crash shortly.[6]

---

6 Hubbard, "Statistical Judgment," Policy Letter of 9 February 1970, *Organization Executive Course*.

CHAPTER 20

LOST PRODUCTION

One must be careful of being led astray by incorrect comparisons.

There is the belief that you can make up for production that didn't occur earlier. This is one of those really strange ideas that we have found in companies all over the world.

In fact, last month's or last week's lost production is gone forever, and there is no way of ever making up for it.

A salesman has a good day, followed by a poor day in which he was not very energetic. So he goes all out to "make up for it" by earning twice as much the next day. "Well, I made up for it," he thinks. He made twice as much on Friday because he didn't make anything on Thursday. But Friday's production belongs to Friday! Friday can't simply loan it to Thursday. What did he do on Friday? Why did he make twice as much on Friday? Why didn't he do that on Thursday? A human being will earn what he thinks he needs in order to survive.

Most individuals or companies are intent on economizing. Save a dollar here, ten dollars there, hundreds or thousands "saved." But, if the company should have been earning fifty thousand a week and is only earning thirty, they are losing twenty thousand dollars a week and will never "save it" into affluence. While saving is important, too much attention is placed on it. *The most money you're ever going to lose is the money you should have made and didn't.* The production lost on Thursday is lost forever. It can never be gotten back. That is the "unreasonable" viewpoint. One never makes up tomorrow what didn't get produced today. Today's lost production is lost forever. And tomorrow's production belongs to tomorrow.

> **But the greater loss to Finance is income lost or never made.**
>
> **The difference between what an organization should be making and what it does gives Finance greater loss than any FP[1] saving could ever recover.[2]**

Expansion needs to be constantly created so that every day is a winner! It really comes down to one's own demand for production. Remember this quotation from Mr. Hubbard:

> **The income potential of any usual group is established by the demand for income, not by any other important factor.**
>
> **In financial supervision on an International basis, this is the only factor one works with. While it is *reasonable* to suppose that income will occur for other reasons and can be achieved in other ways, the actual fact is that only demand by the group produces any income at all.[3]**

HOW OFTEN?

A statistic can be kept hourly, daily, weekly, monthly, yearly, etc. How much stat you keep depends upon how closely you can observe the scene.

> **The closer one is to the scene of the stat, the more rapidly it can be adjusted and the smaller the amount of time per stat needed to interpret it.**

---

1 *FP:* "Financial Planning." Hubbard, *Modern Management Technology Defined.*

2 Hubbard, "Bean Theory, Finance As A Commodity," Policy Letter of 19 March 1971 (Revised and Reissued 27 October 1982), *Management Series.*

3 Hubbard, "Financial Management, Building Fund Account," Policy Letter of 18 January 1965, *Organization Executive Course.*

One can interpret one's own personal statistic hour to hour.

A division head can interpret on a basis of day to day.

A head of a sector (several divisions) needs a few days' worth of stat.

An Executive Director would use a week's worth of stat.

A more remote governing body would use a TREND (which would be several weeks) of divisional stats to interpret.

In short the closer one is to a statistic the easier it is to interpret it and the easier it is to change it.[4]

Many executives or managers should be getting their statistics daily, while some need them weekly and others on a monthly basis. If they're close to the scene and the statistics are reviewed at the end of the week, and they're down, something could have been done about it earlier in the week. Why wait to the end of the week to find out you had poor production? If you wait until the end of the week to make corrections, you aren't going to save any losses. If you don't spot it until the end of the week, you have just blown the whole week. The sooner you can isolate the changes, both the positive changes and negative changes, the better off you are. You won't have to "make up for it next week."

Let's take a telephone solicitor, as an example. His job is to get the people he calls to see an insurance salesman in their home. He might keep a stat every hour. He has a stat of "the number of people who are willing to see a salesman." For the first hour—stats up. He reinforces what he was doing. Next hour stats drop. So he takes a look at it and thinks, "All right, what did I change? I think I was

---

4   Hubbard, "Stat Interpretation," Policy Letter of 3 October 1970, *Organization Executive Course.*

getting hungry, so I speeded up my sales pitch a lot. Yeah, that is what it was. Okay, I'll eat." He knows something changed. So he handles it and stats go up. Later, they drop. He looks. "Well, I'm not doing anything differently—maybe something different in my environment...oh, there is the new telemarketer who is working nearby and this guy is really upsetting the people he is calling...and I think it's upsetting me. I'll move away." He moves away, and his stats go up.

Thus, you might keep stats every half-hour, hour, day, or week. Of course, you don't want to get so interiorized into the game of stats that you don't produce anything, and your job becomes graphing graphs, or your stat is "how many stats I keep." Remember, it is your tool—it's got to be helpful.

PREDICTION

Another important factor of statistics is that they give you the ability to observe current conditions accurately and predict future ones.

"We're doing great" may be just idle comment, not fact. "The company's gross income has gone from $60,000 a week to $90,000 in 6 weeks." But statistics are a subject of comparison. They may be spending $100,000 to make the $90,000! So one graph alone is not significant. You need to compare it to other graphs.

MULTIPLE GRAPHS

One must keep enough graphs to make proper comparisons.

A single datum or subject has to have a datum or subject with which to compare it before it can be fully understood.[5]

---

5 Hubbard, "Breakthroughs," Policy Letter of 12 May 1970, *Organization Executive Course.*

Gross income alone, as a statistic, means nothing if the bills are higher than income.

It is the comparison of statistics that reaps the rewards in staticizing.

Let's take an antique book dealer:

1. Monthly number of books sold is up,

2. Monthly number of calls to prospective buyers is down, and

3. Monthly letters out to prospective customers concerning books is down.

If you were not keeping all three stats, you would never see that his outflow is down. Supposing you had "books sold" as the only stat. You say, "Books sold: up, we are in great shape." But it is likely that stats will be down in the future because the "people contacted regarding books" stat is down, and "letters to buyers" is down. But somehow books are being sold. You want to immediately investigate and find out. And the reasons for doing so are obvious:

> **You can't know what's happening in a kitchen by talking to a cook. Because he's not cooking just then. You can't know how good the food is without tasting it. You don't know really how clean a floor is without wiping at it. You don't know how clean an ice box is without smelling it.[6]**

Look for the change. You might discover that someone had a bright idea earlier and was using a new window sign and it was selling books—but then it got taken down. You put it back up. Even that may not be enough—where was the sign located? Why was it successful? You find out that they put up a display near the college bookstore. Bingo! You reinstate the successful action.

---

6 Hubbard, "Look Don't Listen," Policy Letter of 16 March 1972, *Management Series*.

Let's use a sales organization as another example. In our management consultations, we have discovered that far too many sales organizations operate on an insufficient number of graphs or stats. Usually they will keep a record of total sales and income—as well as the individual sales. Yet there are some valuable indicators (remember, stats are indicators) that ought to be kept as well:

1. The number of phone calls made to prospective customers

2. The number of people spoken to (contacts)

3. The number of actual sales made

4. The dollar amount of the sales

5. Total of actual income received

6. Income divided by the number of sales (average sale)

Now these statistics compared one to the other tell you something of value. Graphs are like flags telling you to take notice of something. And if you look at them in a group, they'll "talk" to you, they give you the whole picture. If the "signals" are seen and the down stat is investigated, we may suddenly find out that the owner got his mailing list from some high school and he's calling people who are sixteen years old and don't want anything to do with false teeth preparation, which is what the company is selling.

But perhaps we've got lots of phone calls being made and lots of people being contacted but still don't have any increased sales. In that case there's probably something wrong with the sales pitch or delivery of it. It's all a matter of comparison. Keeping a running record of production helps ensure continued production and pinpoints where production falters. Proper management relies on stats. Comparing is the heart of it all.

GRAPHING

There is another important, yet often overlooked, cause for graphs not being used: the scale of the graph. By scale is meant a number of anything per vertical inch of graph. You can also get a pattern that looks like it is simply "snaking" along the bottom when the scale or values for the stats you have chosen are incorrect. You can't really evaluate the graph, as the represented changes are too small. You can get the reverse situation where your scale is too big and the graph looks like repeating peaks and valleys.

> **A graph is not informative if its vertical scale results in graph line changes that are too small. It is not possible to draw the graph at all if the line changes are too large.**[7]

A graph is the playing field upon which the game of business is played. Mr. Hubbard details the correct approach as follows:

> **Scale is different for each statistic.**
>
> **1. Determine the lowest amount one expects a particular statistic to go—this is not always zero.**
>
> **2. Determine the highest amount one can believe the statistic will go on the next three months.**
>
> **3. Subtract 1 from 2.**
>
> **4. Proportion the vertical divisions as per 3.**
>
> **Your scale will then be quite real and show up its rises and falls.**[8]

Now you can create a graph (the playing field) that is tailor-made for your game.

---

7 Hubbard, "Statistic Graphs, How To Figure The Scale," Policy Letter of 6 March 1966, *Organization Executive Course.*

8 Hubbard, "Statistic Graphs, How To Figure The Scale."

Let's say you have a graph of twelve weeks. Put dates across the bottom—weekly. Put the amount of income you think you will end up with after a three-month period at the top of the left side (where amounts are listed). Now on the left side, bottom line, put a figure which you know that you won't go below. Subtract the bottom from the top number. Now divide that by 10. The number you get after you make that division is how much value you are going to give to each 10th horizontal line. Mark your income at the close of the week and connect the dots.

When a graph is done properly in this fashion, you've got the right size playing field for your game. The most effective way to record the statistics and graph them properly is to use the Management By Statistics software published by MasterTech.[9] Their highly successful program not only permits the user to easily incorporate management by statistics into their business, but also incorporates many administrative breakthroughs by L. Ron Hubbard on the subject of statistical analysis.

---

9 MasterTech Computer Products International, Inc. Website: www.mastertech.com; email: sales@mastertech.com.

CHAPTER 21

FIXED CONDITIONS VS. EXPANSION

S ome individuals or companies consistently have a flat graph— that is to say, stats that go level across the graph. There are lots of "reasons" usually given as to why it's flat, but they are merely explanations as to why the statistic is down. This applies to any statistic that is down, on a downtrend, or even flat. On Earth, any activity either expands or contracts—it never stays the same.

It is an empirical (observed and proven by observation) fact that nothing remains exactly the same forever. This condition is foreign to this universe. Things grow or they lessen. They cannot apparently maintain the same equilibrium or stability.

Thus things either expand or they contract. They do not remain level in this universe. Further when something seeks to remain level and unchanged it contracts.

Thus we have three actions and only three. First is expansion, second is the effort to remain level or unchanged and third is contraction or lessening.

Given these three actions, the choice is clear:

To survive, then, one must expand as the only safe condition of operation.[1]

1 Hubbard, "Expansion, Theory Of Policy," Policy Letter of 4 December 1966, *Organization Executive Course.*

113

What do you do with a flat graph? Make it go up! "I'm not going to accept this anymore." A good first step.

> **Organizations are not well run by the old school tie[2], what professor one knew in the Ivy League University or who is shacked up with whom. Organizations run by other considerations than stats hurt the individual staff members. Organizations are well run when they are run by fairly and realistically designed stats for every staff member, division and the organization.[3]**

Remember, you are keeping stats for expansion. That is the name of the game.

As an example, here is a graph—$60,000 a week at the top, $10,000 on the bottom.

Stats are up and you end off the quarter at $43,000 for the week. You have not gone below $25,000 during that last quarter. It's time for a new graph. You are going to target the company for $80,000 a week by the end of the next quarter. So there is a new normal which is now about $40,000, which used to be your high.

Today's affluence becomes tomorrow's normal!

If $30,000 is still a "good figure" (even though you've hit it about 20 times), how are you going to expand? Inflation itself is eating up your dollars.

One answer is you've got to increase your level of demand. The salesperson is targeting fifty items sold and you've got to regularly

---

2 *Old school tie:* "The expression *old school tie* has essentially the same meaning as the business association interpretation of old boy network. This expression derives from school ties indicating that the wearer is an old boy of a particular school." Wikipedia.com.

3 Hubbard, "Statistics, Management By," Policy Letter of 5 February 1970, *Organization Executive Course.*

get him up to sixty, seventy, eighty, or 100. Where you can get tripped up is he does 100, then 110, then he goes to sixty and nothing is done about it because, after all, "sixty is much higher than other salesmen are doing." What does that have to do with him? Sixty for this guy is no longer acceptable.

So expansion should be your viewpoint in running your business and your life. And there is a vital formula:

[E]xpansion formula:

DIRECT A CHANNEL TOWARD ATTAINMENT, PUT SOMETHING ON IT, REMOVE DISTRACTIONS, BARRIERS, NONCOMPLIANCE AND OPPOSITION.[4]

Thus we can see that expansion does have some definite rules. Expansion does not simply arrive on its own. This is further highlighted by specific actions for expansion:

1. **PROVIDE GOOD POLICY.**

2. **MAKE IT EASILY KNOWABLE.**

3. **BE STRENUOUS IN MAKING SURE IT IS FOLLOWED.**[5]

It takes hard work and it takes your intention.[6] You make it happen.

You can target statistics being up, which helps create more motivation and willingness. But it would be an error to simply tell people what their targets are, to tell people what their quotas are, without gaining any real agreement.

---

4 Hubbard, "The Structure Of Organization, What Is Policy?" Policy Letter of 13 March 1965, *Organization Executive Course.*

5 See note #4 above.

6 *Intention:* "It's an idea that one is going to accomplish something. It's intentional, which means he *meant* to do it, he *means* to do it." Hubbard, *Technical Dictionary.*

Motivation begins with knowing another person's reality before you can get them motivated towards where you want them to be.

An exec goes to a seminar and gets all pumped up, realizing that the whole trouble with the company is that they are not "thinking big." So he gets all employees together and says, "We've been making 500 widgets a month and I realized that what we should be doing is 1,000." He then attempts to deliver the whole weekend seminar in three minutes. "One thousand widgets a month, that's what we've got to do," he says. And everybody in the audience smiles and says OK, until he leaves the room, at which point they say, "What is he talking about? We are killing ourselves trying to do 500 widgets and he wants 1,000?" He's committed a cardinal sin in motivation—being unreal. Remember, the first four letters of reality are R-E-A-L. The "motor" of motivation is agreement.

You can always work on getting some agreement on what can be done. How about 750 widgets? Is that real? Does everyone agree with that? Well, how about 700? All right, at 700 we get group agreement. Getting employees to agree that something is do-able, achievable, within reach, is a very valuable tool of management. But that is not the end of motivation. It is not sufficient simply to have everyone with a positive concept. I'm totally in favor of positive thinking: I know that my house will not be burglarized. But I also lock the door! What is going to occur to make sure that we actually reach 700? What tangible things are going to be done? The positive concept is terrific. But it must be backed up with some action. Positive thinking along with positive action! We know where we're going, how we're going to get there, and what we are going to do when we arrive: the reward.

Chapter 22

The Ideal Scene

Now that we have covered PRODUCTS (VFPs), and how many products we are getting in how much time (STATS), let's go to IDEAL SCENE(S).

Mr. Hubbard defines Ideal Scene as:

> **The state of affairs envisioned by policy or the improvement of even that.[1]**

Policy and procedures are written to establish an ideal operating environment so that things will run smoothly and effectively. What it would look like if the office, company or specific aspects of the operation were running well, would be an ideal scene.

Every activity you engage in should have an IDEAL SCENE created for it.

How do you measure how well you are surviving? How do you know if something is not optimum? You have to compare the existing scene to something better—the ideal scene for that activity.

Where do you think your operation should be so that you can measure it against where it is now? The ideal scene versus the existing scene.

---

1 Hubbard, "Handling: Policy, Plans, Programs, Projects and Orders Defined," Policy Letter of 29 February 1972, *Organization Executive Course.*

An incorrect comparison can often turn out to be a form of reasonableness or a justification for not being closer to the ideal scene. Again, "I'm not too healthy but I'm a lot healthier than that wino in the gutter." The comparison should actually be your ideal state of health as measured (measured in stats) against your existing state of health!

KEEPING IT REAL

One must also consider how much of the ideal scene can be achieved and how soon. The ideal being mocked up must fit with the actual scene being looked at and not some other imagined scene or any particular personal wish for the activity.

For example, if we were to open a fruit stand on downtown Main Street, the ideal scene would not be "to own the building behind me," as it would be unreal for the activity of opening a fruit stand on Main Street. The actual ideal scene might be something like "an attractive fruit stand, profitably run with good fresh fruit sold at economical prices. An ever-increasing number of customers who come back daily and tell their friends, resulting in a need for more space—an addition onto the stand or even another stand down the block, etc."

An ideal scene must be connected to reality.

Envisioning an attainable future requires some connection with reality.

There is no harm at all in dreaming wonderful dreams for the future. It's almost the bread of life.

But how about giving oneself a crashing failure by disconnecting from any reality?

Some laborers do this to themselves. Taking no steps to attain it, they daydream themselves as kings or some other grand identity. Well, all right. But that isn't an

"Ideal Scene". That's a delusion engaged upon for self gratification in a dream world.

One can not only dream a *possible* Ideal Scene but he *can* attain it.

So an Ideal Scene is SOMETHING THAT CAN BE ATTAINED.

It should be quite real.[2]

This same viewpoint applies to getting better production volume as well. One must set real targets:

Some people setting unreal quotas are really setting some impossible Ideal Scene. "Complete this work in 1 hour!" to someone working hard on a job that will take 4 days is delusory. It is setting, without saying so, the Ideal Scene of having a worker who is really a magician! The here and now is a guy sweating it out and trying. And that's an Ideal Scene that is missed![3]

Observe what *should be there*, and match it up to *what is there* at any given time. The IDEAL SCENE is a tool you can use when something is not going right (or to verify a rightness) by comparing the two scenes.

Sometimes we accept the existing scene unquestioningly as the ideal simply because "it has been that way for so long."

Too often what is "normal" is fully accepted without inspection. What was considered at one time as ideal gets whittled down by life, each day a bit more, an erosion of an ideal until "normal" is acceptable. As mentioned earlier, by using the dimmer switch on a

---

2 Hubbard, "Envisioning The Ideal Scene," Policy Letter of 11 August 1974, *Management Series.*

3 See note #2 above.

room light switch I could dim the room light just a bit. And pretty soon the light level is pretty low—but it's now "normal." Where has the original brightness gone? We let it slip away; we allowed the dimness to occur, slowly but surely, in the name of "that's life"— "that's normal."

When you've got the ideal scene correctly envisioned, if there is an oddity (by comparison), you can spot it right away as it stands out against the ideal. You have an ideal scene against which to compare what you're looking at. And what doesn't compare stands out.

If you start looking at what the ideal scene might or should be, the existing scene gets a comparison and one begins to gain clarity of observation.

Your ideal scene should not have a "fixed idea" or have any "oddities" in it. If it does, when you compare it to the existing scene and the existing scene has a similar "oddity," you will not spot the oddity as such—it will simply appear that everything is fine. This is a vital piece of technology for proper observation.

A fixed idea is something accepted without personal inspection or agreement. It is the perfect "authority knows best". It is the "reliable source". A typical one was the Intelligence report accepted by the whole US Navy right up to 7 Dec. 1941, the date of destruction of the US fleet by Japanese planes. The pre-Pearl Harbor report, from unimpeachably reliable sources was "the Japanese cannot fly—they have no sense of balance". The report overlooked that the Japanese were the world's greatest acrobats! It became a fixed idea that caused the neglect of all other reports.

A fixed idea is uninspected. It blocks the existence of any contrary observation.

Most reactionaries (people resisting all progress or action) are suffering from fixed ideas which they received from "authorities", which no actual experience alters.

That British red-coated infantry never took cover was another one. It took a score or two of wars and fantastic loss of life to finally break it down. If any single fixed idea destroyed the British Empire, this one is a candidate.[4]

You can see that not "taking cover" had nothing to do with the purpose of winning wars and was far from an ideal scene! Thus, the ideal scene you envision must connect to the purpose of the activity.

As an example, Joe is a sales supervisor. We inquire as to his ideal scene and we get: "More and more salesmen working every week, making more and more money. Of course, I'm working seven days a week, because you have to watch the salesmen all the time." By querying this somewhat odd statement we find that Joe has "unethical salesmen" unknowingly as part of his ideal scene and that is why they have to be watched. So he thinks when the salesmen are cheating or stealing, that's "normal,"and his solution was to "watch the salesmen all the time."

Joe didn't work out the IDEAL SCENE for his activity. He is accepting whatever the existing scene is as "normal." And while Joe thinks he is doing great, he is declining in the statistics of the other areas of his life. Why? Because his ideal scene does not include "ethical salesman who can operate on their own, and do so." That is not any part of it. If it were, he would spot unethical salesmen in his existing scene as an oddity immediately.

---

4 Hubbard, "Sanity," Policy Letter of 19 May 1970, *Management Series.*

If the sales supervisor had an Ideal Scene as above or added "salesmen who are ethical and can be trusted, while I work less hours for more money, train other people to take my place and go up the company ladder, etc.," he'd be surviving a lot better. Oddities exist in his ideal scene, and that's the trouble. The ideal scene should be free of oddities, points that do not add up, which Mr. Hubbard calls "outpoints."

> **Whenever an observer himself has fixed ideas he tends to look at them not at the information.**[5]

You should be constantly striving to bring the existing scene up to the ideal scene. Then when it's achieved, you put a new ideal scene there, and sometimes even work out a whole new admin scale.

---

5 Hubbard, "Sanity."

CHAPTER 23

PURPOSE AND IDEAL SCENE

P urpose is directly related to the ideal scene.

The entire concept of an Ideal Scene for any activity is really a clean statement of its PURPOSE.[1]

With this optimum standard in mind, one could measure any existing scene against the ideal and immediately see what needed attention. Any departure from the ideal would then stand out. So your ideal scene has to be sane and it has to be the ideal scene for what you're looking at. That's why graphs are so useful. To put $20,000 on the top of a graph is someone's imagination if the person is making $200 a week. When you have that kind of over-reaching, it is really hope, or a "fixed idea," not an ideal scene.

The difference between the existing scene and the ideal scene should not be too great. In such a case, it might mean that the ideal scene is unreal and you have to bring it down a little bit. Or you have to get more unreasonable about it and work harder to achieve the ideal scene.

THE OMITTED IDEAL SCENE

Sometimes the entire concept of the ideal scene is missing. Employees lacking in experience in a particular area will often have a

---

1 Hubbard, "How To Find And Establish An Ideal Scene," Policy Letter of 5 July 1970, *Management Series*.

hard time envisioning what the ideal scene really is. As a result, their seniors have a hard time, as the employees don't see the same ideal scene they do.

> **The offices neat and orderly might not even be imagined by someone who has seen them in a mess for two years. He may think that's the way they're supposed to be! And be quite incapable of envisioning the offices in any other condition!**
>
> **Thus, if one cannot see the offices should be clean, he does not see that they are dirty and messy as a *Situation*. Thus when he is told the public won't come into the place, and even if he finds the place is full of old dirty junk, he can't evaluate it as a clean orderly place would not be envisioned by him. So he doesn't get "dirty place" as a valuable datum, doesn't get "A clean orderly place that is inviting to the public" as an Ideal Scene, doesn't get "Office so dirty the public won't go near it" as a Situation and so cannot find a Why[2] to lack of public! And so as he didn't find *Why* it was so dirty and disorderly, it wouldn't handle.[3]**

OBSERVATION

Observational abilities improve when one practices working out an ideal scene. It also keeps you unreasonable, because now you've got a standard of unreasonability. You refuse to invent reasons for the down stat.

---

2 *Why:* "The real reason found by the investigation." Hubbard, *Modern Management Technology Defined.*

3 Hubbard, "Envisioning The Ideal Scene," Policy Letter of 11 August 1974, *Management Series.*

Often, a failure to create an accurate ideal scene stems from an inability to confront some kind of oddity. Instead of confronting it, there is a tendency to either avoid the area or invent reasons why it is less than optimum. Hubbard called this:

> **Law of the Omitted Data:**
>
> **Where there is no data available people will invent it.**[4]

And here's why:

> **Illogic occurs when one or more data is misplaced into the wrong body of data for it.**
>
> **An example would be "Los Angeles smog was growing worse so we fined New York." That is pretty obviously a misplace.**
>
> **"Cars were no longer in use. Bacterial warfare had taken its toll."**
>
> **"I am sorry madam but you cannot travel first class on a third class passport."**
>
> **Humanoid response to such displacements is to be *reasonable*. A new false datum is dreamed up and put into the body of data to explain why that datum is included.**
>
> **A reasonable person would accept a pig in a parlor by imagining that there was a good reason for it. And leave the pig in the parlor and revise their *own* ideal scene!**[5]

---

4 "Law of the Omitted Data" (definition), Hubbard, *Modern Management Technology Defined.*

5 Hubbard, "The Missing Scene," Policy Letter of 23 June 1970, *Management Series.*

CREATING THE IDEAL SCENE

L. Ron Hubbard gives a considerable number of guidelines to ensure that the Ideal Scene created is a correct one.

LOSING ONE'S WAY

One's direction is lost to the degree one fails to work out the Ideal Scene.

It is so easy to toss off an "ideal scene" that is not *the* Ideal Scene that one can begin with a false premise.

As he tries to work with an incorrect "ideal scene" for an activity he may fail and grow discouraged without recognizing that he is already working with an omitted datum—the *real* Ideal Scene for that activity.[6]

To ensure you do have a real ideal scene, you can measure it by stats. Stats are derived from the ideal scene. When stats are going up, you are getting closer to the ideal scene. In the same issue, he cautions:

To suppose one can instantly hit upon an Ideal Scene for any activity without further test is to be very fond of one's own prejudices.

There is however, a test of whether you have the Ideal Scene or not.

Can you staticize it?. . .

Whatever the facts and economic rules may be about production and the Ideal Scene, it would seem to be the case, sufficient at least for our purposes, that this rule holds good:

---

6 Hubbard, "Irrationality," Policy Letter of 6 July 1970, *Management Series.*

THE CORRECTLY STATED IDEAL SCENE WILL HAVE A PRODUCTION STATISTIC.[7]

Working out the ideal scene can take a bit of confronting. What is part of this ideal scene? Am I missing anything? I have also found that what you might tend to leave out of your ideal scene is what might not be working too well for you in a particular activity. I have worked with executives who no longer track or measure their profit, as there had not been any for some time. Then, when postulating their ideal scene, profit is actually omitted (they're so used to not having any). This area has not been confronted or handled, so it is omitted from the ideal scene.

Here's a sample of a telephone salesperson's ideal scene:

"Having a good list of potential prospects to call; knowing when to call (best time); reaching an ever-increasing number of people, who are willing to listen to my sales talk; a good script delivered in a tone of voice that keeps their interest—resulting in an increasing number of sales, which stay sold through timely delivery of a high-quality product, with a viable commission paid to me."

Note the many stats we can evolve from this:

OF CALLS MADE

OF CONTACTS OF POTENTIAL BUYERS

OF SALES

OF PAID DELIVERIES

GROSS SALES VOLUME

OF HOURS WORKED COMPARED TO GROSS SALES VOLUME

$ AMOUNT OF PERSONAL INCOME

---

7 Hubbard, "Irrationality."

Another aspect of the ideal scene from the point of view of this salesman might be the comparison stat: hours spent selling against how much he personally makes.

There might be a production stat of $10,000 gross sales, but if the number of hours to get it keeps rising, it would not be ideal. Thus, we can back it up with a stat.

COMPARISONS

We often see another form of incorrect comparison demonstrated by people who are very able. They sometimes measure their own production and progress only by comparison to others in their organization or field rather than against their own potential production.

This is sometimes seen in the form of an employee who needs to be told constantly to get his or her production up—and does so every time. After a while, one gets the idea that this person can push that stat up almost at will—and if you get into communication with him, you will soon find out that this is actually the case. He's monitoring his production by what others, with perhaps less ability, are producing. The pressure or demand for greater production is not self-generated as it should be, but must come from his seniors. The solution, in such a case, is to get into communication with him about it and to set targets that are a game (challenge) for him—without consideration of anyone else's level of production. You may be surprised when the production of others around him increases.

Practice envisioning ideal scenes for any activity. The next time you go into to a restaurant, take a look and conceptualize what the Ideal Scene for that restaurant would be: "waiters busily working, clean plates, fast service, etc." And when you walk in, you will probably observe things that you have never seen before.

The idea of setting an ideal scene and comparing the existing scene against it is an observation drill, and a very important one.

It is an ability that one develops by practice, by experience, and by looking at an area and setting the ideal scene.

Ideally a Valuable Product

The ideal scene should be directly related to the product, and it should be a valuable product as well. You must be dealing with an ethical and effective product, which is exchangeable for a fair price.

Working out the Ideal Scene in harmony with the VFP can cause tremendous changes in one's viewpoint and how one goes about living.

Creating the Ideal Scene on any aspect of life is a vital action and will lead to greater productivity and increased morale.

Indeed, there are areas of your business, if not areas of your life, that could be improved simply by working out what the ideal is for that scene and comparing it to the existing scene. If your special relationship or marriage, for instance, is not going too well, work out what the ideal scene should be, match it against the existing scene and, measuring the two, see what has to be done to bring the existing closer to the ideal. Ideal scenes are a valuable tool to be used for expansion.

Summary

A VFP is something that has to be of high quality. Find your publics. Create a demand for the product. Put it into the hands of your publics. Get your exchange.

Track how well you are doing with STATISTICS, comparing them to other statistics. And stay on course through the use of the IDEAL SCENE.

The next level concerns how to move from where you are up to where you want to be. This area is called PLANNING.

If you have a rather large distance between the ideal scene and the existing scene, do not be discouraged. The next level of this Scale of Importances will assist you in bringing your existing scene to your ideal scene.

The difference between the ideal scene and the existing scene is handled with the tools of PLANNING.

CHAPTER 24

PLANNING

How quickly you are going to get from your existing scene to your ideal scene will depend upon this section of the Admin Scale covering PLANS, PROGRAMS, PROJECTS, and ORDERS. All of these points fall under the heading of PLAN-NING.

Mr. Hubbard defines plans as:

> **The general bright idea one has to . . . get things up to the ideal scene or improve even that.[1]**

He further defines the other key points of planning as:

> **The program is the big solution to a problem—the big problem is solved by a big solution called a program. The little problems inside that big solution are solved by projects. And inside the projects the littler problems are solved by orders.[2]**

Raising statistics and producing more valuable final products is done by planning, and planning takes **confront**[3], a prerequisite to successful planning (and doing!).

---

1 "Plan" (definition), Hubbard, Modern Management Technology Defined, from Policy Letter of 29 Feb. 1972, Issue II, *Management Series.*

2 "Project" (definition), Hubbard, *Modern Management Technology Defined.*

3 *Confront*: "direct observation." Hubbard, *Modern Management Technology Defined.*

GRADIENTS

Confronting this subject of planning or programming is really a subject of gradients.[4] Just about anything can be confronted if it is broken down into gradients.

> **The source of most failures. . . . Either too shallow or too steep** [a gradient].[5]

An order such as "You must renovate a hotel this week. Please have it done by next Wednesday" would be overwhelming. It is also probably not going to get done. If you run your operation on orders alone. Without a plan, program or project, you will not have a very smooth and expanding operation. Lots of those "undone orders" probably didn't get done because they were not confrontable as one single item or command.

An order might be in the category of "Pick up that chair." "Shut off the light." "Go downstairs." These are orders.

And where do orders come from? Orders are derived from projects. Not just from some arbitrary idea.

Projects come out of programs. A program is broader than a project. Where did the program come from? It came from a plan. Thus, these are gradient steps to accomplish the ideal scene.

PLANNING: POLICY, PURPOSES AND GOALS

And the plans come from the Admin Scale level above it—POLICY—defined as:

---

4 *Gradient Scale:* "[A] gradual increasing degree of something. A non-gradient scale would be telling someone to enter a skyscraper by a 32nd-story window." Hubbard, *Modern Management Technology Defined.*

5 Hubbard, "Gradients and ARC," 1 September 1966, Saint Hill Special Briefing Course Lecture 442 (Level I.).

The rules of the game, the facts of life, the discovered truths and the invariable procedures.[6]

An example of policy consistent with a plan might be: "Each year, the revenue of the company will be reviewed and the areas that showed the highest increase in revenue will have a complete financial analysis done. The strong points found in this analysis will be reinforced the next year." That is the policy. The analysis revealed that conventions pulled 50% more income than they did the last year and had a considerable increase in profit. Thus, the plan— "Increase Conventions"—is consistent with policy.

The policy, of course, comes out of the next level of the scale, PURPOSE(S) of the company. (You wouldn't have a POLICY of reviewing the revenue categories if you didn't have PURPOSES that had something to do with expansion.)

PURPOSE: The lesser goal applying to specific activities or subjects.[7]

Purpose could also be looked at as the route chosen for survival.

And, of course, the purpose(s) come out of the goal(s), which are the broad, overall objectives.

GOAL: A known objective toward which an action is directed with the purpose of achieving that end.[8]

A hotel company's purposes and goals might be:

"PURPOSES: To provide temporary housing for businesspersons living within and visiting our city, at a profit to our company.

---

6 "Policy" (definition), Hubbard, *Modern Management Technology Defined.*

7 "Purpose" (definition), Hubbard, *Modern Management Technology Defined.*

8 "Goal" (definition), Hubbard, *Modern Management Technology Defined.*

"GOALS: To be the leading hotelier in the city, providing practical and aesthetic hotel spaces at a profit in which communication and commerce are encouraged, and provide for and establish an increasingly healthy economy for our city residents and businesses."

Thus we can see that there is a sequence in the SCALE OF IMPORTANCE. L. Ron Hubbard makes this sequence very clear in the definition of Scale of Importance:

> **Top is a *goal*, next is a *purpose*, next is a *policy*, then you have a *plan* then you have a *program* then you have a *project* and now you have an *order* then you have an *ideal scene* and then you have a *statistic* and then you have a *valuable final product*. That is the scale of importance. Now of course anybody can issue an order if there is a project which is derived from a program which is derived from a plan which is directly derived from policy. Policy is no good unless it is derived from a purpose. Skip having any plan at all if it doesn't eventually wind up in a valuable final product. Do you see that there's a band here? It's a band of dwindling authority but it also moves forward down the lines.[9]**

The following are important planning definitions:

> **PLANNING: A systematic way of thinking in which ideas are arranged in orderly outline taking an endeavor from present time onward to a given point or conclusion, and which may encompass either short or long range goals.[10]**

> **PLANS: Short range broad intentions as to the contemplated actions envisaged for the handling of a broad area to remedy it or expand it or to obstruct or impede an**

---

9 "Scale of Importance" (definition), Hubbard, *Modern Management Technology Defined.*

10 "Planning" (definition), Hubbard, *Modern Management Technology Defined.*

opposition to expansion. A plan is usually based on observation of potentials (or resources) and expresses a bright idea of how to use them.[11]

All manner of plans can be drawn and can be okayed. ... A *plan* would be the *design* of the thing itself.[12]

PROGRAM: A series of steps in sequence to carry out a plan.[13]

The program is the big solution to a problem. ... The little problems inside that big solution are solved by projects. And inside the projects the littler-littler problems are solved by orders.[14]

PROJECTS: The sequence of steps written to carry out ONE step of a Program. Project orders often have to be written to execute a Program step. ... These are a series of GUIDING STEPS which if followed will result in a full and successful accomplishment of the Program Target.[15]

ORDERS: The verbal or written direction from a lower or designated authority to carry out a program step or apply the general policy. ... Some program steps are so simple that they are themselves an order or an order can simply be a roughly written project. ... The program step itself or the verbal or written project to get the Program step fully *Done*.[16]

---

11 Hubbard, "Handling: Policy, Plans, Programs, Projects and Orders Defined," Policy Letter of 29 February 1972, *Management Series*.

12 Hubbard, "Planning and Targets," Policy Letter of 18 January 1969, *Organization Executive Course*.

13 See note #11 above.

14 "Project" (definition), Hubbard, *Modern Management Technology Defined.*

15 Hubbard, "Handling: Policy, Plans, Programs, Projects and Orders Defined."

CREATING AND IMPLEMENTING PROGRAMS

A Program was previously defined as:

A series of steps in sequence to carry out a plan.[17]

The chief executive officer of the hotel, per hotel policy, checked the revenue. He found that the hotel had 50% more profit from conventions than the previous year. He would not then send this information in a note to someone in the hotel and simply order them to "get hotel convention business up 400% this year!" It's doubtful this would get done. Too many moving parts. "Well, I'm the president, let them figure it out" is not a pro-survival attitude either. It would end up in someone's in-basket for six months because it was not confrontable. And when he finds out that nothing has been done, does he again "order" it to be done immediately? If the original order was overwhelming, why would the "nudge order" be effective? It would not. So what should be done? Some strategy should be developed and a plan written to increase convention business 400% this year! You've got to create the plan so programs or a program can be written for the plan steps.

The objective of this plan is to "Increase the convention business by 400%."

There are going to be several broad steps involved (PROGRAMS) and completed in sequence. Each major action listed to complete the plan is a program step of the plan. Each sub-action (A to H) is a project created to complete the program step, and orders will be listed as needed to complete projects. A sample follows:

---

16 "Project" (definition), Hubbard, *Modern Management Technology Defined.*

17 See note #16 above.

PLAN—Increase the convention business by 400% by (date)

1. RENOVATE THE EAST WING

Date of Completion

_____ A. Obtain and compile all existing blueprints of hotel. (Foreman) ____

_____ B. Review all blueprints with engineers and architects. (VP) ____

_____ C. Get plan of renovation and upgrade drawn up. (VP) ____

_____ D. Get plan approved. (VP) ____

_____ E. Create a financial estimate of work that needs
to be done. (Controller) ____

_____ F. Choose contractors (would include all aspects of
contracting work to be done, estimates and bids, etc.)
(Controller) ____

_____ G. Submit all needed financing to Board of Directors.(Controller) ____

_____ H. Begin renovations. (Foreman) ____

(More program steps might then follow to fully complete all renovations.) While the renovations are taking place, other major actions would be happening such as marketing.

2. MARKETING

_____ A. Develop marketing campaign. (Marketing Dir) ____

_____ B. Compile or obtain new or current convention

group lists. (Marketing Dir)____

_____ C. Survey and promote to such lists. (Marketing Dir)____

_____ D. Promote Grand Opening. (Marketing Dir)____

The president would send the plan ("broad intentions") to those who are responsible for getting the work done. As it is specifically assigned, those assigned would then have a good idea of what to do. The vice president could get this programmed further and could add his own creativity and initiative.

Note that it usually takes a breakdown of the larger actions into smaller gradient steps to get it all done. Often, program steps themselves need further break-down in the form of a project for ease of accomplishment.As indicated earlier:

> **PROJECTS: The sequence of steps written to carry out ONE step of a Program. Project orders often have to be written to execute a Program step.**
>
> **These are a series of GUIDING STEPS which if followed will result in a full and successful accomplishment of the Program Target.[18]**
>
> **If something requires more than two weeks to do it is a project.[19]**

TEAMWORK

Steps should be dated. Having a date forces in better organization and coordination, helps keep it real.

Be sure when setting a date that once a date is set and calculated, it can actually be done by that date. Once you set that date, that's it. If you leave yourself the "option" of changing the date, then to that degree you are "flinching" already. Dates give us coordination, teamwork, and efficiency.

CERTAINTY

Knowing the direction in which you want to go and fully confronting every step is a surefire way to get there. *Anything can be confronted if you break it down into smaller, more confrontable parts.* A well thought-out and sequenced program or plan is like a certificate of

---

18 Hubbard, "Handling: Policy, Plans, Programs, Projects and Orders Defined."

19 "Projects" (definition), Hubbard, *Modern Management Technology Defined.*

certainty. Then it is simply a matter of how you organize to get it all done. The planning aspect is the preparation and the event is the achieving of your objective. What's more, your planning is done away from the "noise" of life. It is not being done "off the cuff."

If you want a little help in terms of being "unreasonable," this is your commitment. You know exactly where you are going. Nobody can "sell" you just any idea—you won't buy it, as it has nothing to do with your programs. You've already figured out that this is what has to be done, how you are going to do it, and by when.

And by such advance planning, improved efficiency is created. All the extra steps, not to mention unnecessary expenditures, time, etc., are cut out through the use of planning.

Staff time is very often wasted by the failure to use a program-project system.

Example: Department of Promotion and Marketing does a full layout for promotion. Then finds it is against policy, and it isn't used. Means wasted work.

Example: Client administrator is ordered to make a huge board to give client addresses. After a lot of work, it is never used.

WHY? The job never had any part of a program in the first place. It was not part of any general activity. Thus, it is not part of a team action.[20]

Now this doesn't mean that if opportunity presents itself you turn it down because your program doesn't allow you to do it. You are in charge.

---

20 Hubbard, "Programs, Use Of," Policy Letter of 19 August 1971, *Organization Executive Course.*

. . . [I]f these points are grasped, then one sees the scope of the subject and can become quite brilliant and achieve things hitherto out of reach or never thought of before.[21]

Thus we can see that through the use of planning, we can achieve the definition of management as follows:

Management could be said to be the planning of means to attain goals and their assignation for execution to staff and the proper coordination of activities within the group to attain maximal efficiency with minimal effort to attain determined goals.[22]

---

21 Hubbard, "Planning and Targets," Policy Letter of 18 January 1969, *Organization Executive Course.*

22 Hubbard, *How to Live Though an Executive.*

CHAPTER 25

RESOURCES

R esources have a lot to do with how soon you are going to achieve your goals and with how much effort.

What are your resources? You've got a certain level of knowledge, X amount of money in the bank, Y number of employees, Z amount of time, etc. You might have a fantastic project lined up but the staff you have right now are too tied up and are not going to get it done. So what is the solution? You could drop the project until later or hire other people. All these points go into planning.

Before one begins the PLANNING and TARGETING, the resources one has must be considered.

How quickly you move from your existing scene to your IDEAL SCENE will depend upon the bright utilization of resources.

> **Handling must be WITHIN THE CAPABILITIES of those who will do the actions.**
>
> **Handling must be WITHIN THE RESOURCES AVAILABLE.**
>
> **Handling quite often but not always requires a BRIGHT IDEA. It is peculiarly true that the less the resources available the brighter the idea required to attain effective handling.**[1]

---

1 Hubbard, "Proper Format and Correct Action," Policy Letter of 17 February 1972, *Management Series.*

If you wanted to go to China, and had plenty of money, no problem. Just buy the ticket. But suppose one did not have the money, suppose one had little money at all and still wanted to go to China? One would have to get pretty bright! "Who do I know? Does anyone that I know also know some people from China, or who know people in China? I'll make a list of all of the possible resources I have that might help me get to China. And on the list of resources is my ability to speak English! Also on the list was my close association with the owner of the Chinese laundry down the block. What if I speak to him about teaching the rest of his family English? They are still in China and he wants to bring them over next year. In exchange, he will provide a ticket and my room and board in China for the next year." And what do you know? Goodbye Toledo, hello Hong Kong!

Planning always considers resources first.

Every now and then I'm challenged about how planning things so "specifically" seems to take the "fun" out of life. But simply because one plans, does not mean there will be no further surprises. To think so would be folly and an underestimation of the unpredictable adventures on planet Earth. If I am going to Hawaii, I don't want my luggage sent to Japan. What I *can* control, I wish to control. Life still offers up lots of surprises to keep it interesting.

CHAPTER 26

PROGRAMMING

There are some basic principles or maxims[1] concerning PRO-GRAMMING.

These are some of the principles about programs. . . . If you don't know these facts of life, here they are:

MAXIM ONE: Any idea no matter if badly executed is better than no idea at all.

MAXIM TWO: A program to be effective must be executed.

MAXIM THREE: A program put into action requires guidance.

MAXIM FOUR: A program running without guidance will fail and is better left undone. If you haven't got the time to guide it, don't do it; put more steam behind existing programs because it will flop.

MAXIM FIVE: Any program requires some finance. Get the finance into sight before you start to fire, or have a solid guarantee that the program will produce finance before you execute it.

MAXIM SIX: A program requires attention from somebody. An untended program that is everybody's child will become a juvenile delinquent.

---

1 Maxim: "statement of a general truth." *The World Book Dictionary.*

MAXIM SEVEN: The best program is the one that will reach the greatest number and will do the greatest good on the greatest number. . . .

MAXIM EIGHT: Programs must support themselves financially.

MAXIM NINE: Programs must ACCUMULATE interest and bring in other assistance by *the* virtue of the program interest alone or *they* will never grow.

MAXIM TEN: A program is a bad program if it detracts from programs which are already *proving successful* or distracts staff people or associates from work they are already *doing that* is adding up to successful execution of other programs.[2]

It is important to review your plans against these points.

A BALANCE

While you want to provide for a challenge in your planning, the steps shouldn't be overwhelming. They shouldn't be underwhelming either. A program with forty-three steps may just be too tedious, whereas one with three steps is too brief. And remember that gradients are the key.

You can even raise an organization by gradients so as not to overwhelm it. Set and *make* small targets. Then bigger and bigger ones.

Well, you get the idea.

It's the organization's road to causativeness.[3]

---

2 Hubbard, "Programming," Policy Letter of 23 October 1969, *Organization Executive Course.*

3 Hubbard, "Target Series 1," Policy Letter of 14 January 1969, *Organization Executive Course.*

Review your company activity (or aspects of your life) and look at your existing scene/ideal scene section to determine the overall objective that you are trying to achieve in your position with your company or in life. That is the PLAN MAJOR TARGET.

Give it a PLAN NAME and then list out the broad PLAN steps that will be necessary to achieve it. The completed date is marked as a blank on the right side. List who is assigned the target for execution.

Chapter 27

Coordination

Planning has to be consistent with the valuable final products, ideal scene and stats. In fact, as previously stated, planning must align up and down the scale.

This scale is worked up and worked down UNTIL IT IS (EACH ITEM) IN FULL AGREEMENT WITH THE REMAINING ITEMS.

In short, for success all these items in the scale must agree with all other items in the scale on the same subject.[1]

Real planning creates stability of application and greater certainty. It also helps to keep you "unreasonable" and allows you to go from A to B and ignore interference. And it provides better focus.

It was said that when Cicero spoke, there was always great applause and a standing ovation. But when Demosthenes spoke, the response was "Let's march." That's what good programming based on realistic assessments is all about. Plans properly created can get everyone marching.

---

1 Hubbard, Policy Letter of 6 December 1970, Personnel Series 13, *Management Series*.

CHAPTER 28

POLICY

Plans are derived from POLICY, the Admin Scale level above planning. Policy is defined as:

A rule or procedure or a guidance which permits the basic purpose to succeed.[1]

You can easily see how policy fits in with the more senior level of the Admin Scale, PURPOSES. You know something is good policy if it helps the purpose of the company. If it doesn't, if it hinders the purpose, it's a bad policy. It's as simple as that.

We could consider purpose as a road moving towards a goal. And the sides of the road are policy. It keeps one on the road.

There are several other important definitions of policy:

Long range truths or facts which are not subject to change expressed as operational rules or guides.

The rules of the game, the facts of life, the discovered truths and the invariable procedures.[2]

Given the above definition, "All employees will use the west entrance" is not really a policy as it's subject to change. A policy is very high on the Scale of Importances. From policy we get plans and programs.

---

1 "Policy" (definition), Hubbard, *Modern Management Technology Defined.*

2 See note #1 above.

The guiding principles of an operation are assigned the status of policy. If policy is lacking, then you can see that a key element of your Admin Scale is missing.

Policy has to be issued, it has to be clear and it has to be enforced. If policy is not in writing, it needs to be put in writing, and it needs to be made known to all concerned.

There are additional key definitions of policy, which distinguish it from all other company guidelines.

Policy as a word has many definitions in current dictionaries amongst which only one is partially correct: "a definite course or method of action to guide and determine future decisions." It is also "prudence or wisdom," "a course of action," and a lot of other things, according to the dictionary. It even is said to be laid down at the top. Therefore the word has so many other meanings that the language itself has become confused. Yet, regardless of dictionary fog, the word means an exact thing in the specialized field of management and organization. Policy means the principle evolved and issued by top management for a specific activity to guide planning and programming and authorize the issuance of projects by executives which in turn permit the issuance and enforcement of orders that direct the activity of personnel in achieving production and viability. Policy is therefore a principle by which the conduct of affairs can be guided.

A policy is the law on which orders are authorized and originated.

All policies actually derive in greater or lesser degree from group experience which more or less adds up to group agreement and policies which tend to stay along are actually formed with group agreement and are therefore not outside the perimeter of the group.

Policy is the broad general outline originated by top management. Orders are the instructions issued by the next lower level of management to get things done that result in products.

Policy is a growing thing, based on "what has worked." What works *well* today becomes tomorrow's policy.

The sense in which we use policy is the rules and administrative formulas by which we agree on action and conduct our affairs.

A method of bringing about agreement and communication along certain matters which lead to a higher level of survival. They lead to a higher level of survival if they are good policies, they lead to a lower level of survival if they are poor policies and they lead to complete disaster if they are bad policies.[3]

Policy came from years and years of experience. It's the know-how of handling organizations and groups.

That is what makes the team. It is simply the extant agreement and if there isn't an extant agreement then you have individualized action.[4]

You can see from the above definitions why "company policy" would not include "all employees will use the west entrance." The policy might be more like, "Security will be kept at all times by all employees." This would be more on the line of the "rules of the game" or the "discovered truths, not subject to change."

There must be a distinction between policy and orders. If everything is a policy, then all communications take on a monotone of importance:

---

3   "Policy" (definition), Hubbard, *Modern Management Technology Defined.*

4   See note #3 above.

Policy: "All employees must use the west entrance."

Policy: "Be nice to customers."

Now what happens? People start using the west entrance because it's not really that important and the west entrance is more convenient. Because people are seen using the west entrance, that makes it "okay" not to be nice to customers too! If you violate one policy, you can violate another. Policy has to have an exalted position. It's inviolate. It's the rules of the game.

As Policy is so high up on the Admin Scale, it is not surprising that it creates a major effect on an organization.

A long-established Hubbard management technology policy is **"If it isn't written, it isn't true."**[5] Thus, your operation or activity, no matter how small, must contain the key operating policies in writing.

Additionally, how can you affix responsibility without having the "laws" in writing?

Write your policies; make sure they are easily understood; and require staff to attest in writing that they have read, that they understand, and that they accept responsibility for each policy that affects them or their job duties. Now you can enforce accountability.

If it's verbal data, you will spend an inordinate amount of time having to tell somebody something again and again and again. It's got to be in writing..

By providing good policy, you save time in the long run. Time can and must be created for employee enhancement and per the

---

5 Hubbard, "How To Defeat Verbal Tech Checklist," Policy Letter of 9 February 1979, *Organization Executive Course.*

"IMPORTANT NOTE" in the beginning of the book, employees must understand the words in the policy. By providing the fundamental rules and the time to study and learn them, you are empowering your employee to action as he knows the "rules of the game." If it is important, schedule it. It's important to ensure that not only is there enhancement but that some time is set aside for it. Isn't it interesting that we never seem to have the time to do it right, but we always find the time to do it over?

And the policy must be authorized.

> **The exact mechanism of group or organization aberration is the conflict of COUNTER POLICY.**

> **Illegal policy set at unauthorized levels jams the actions of a group and IS responsible for the inactivity, non-production or lack of team spirit.**[6]

Thus, without authorized policy made known, it gets invented!

> **When no policy at all exists random policy occurs.**

> **When policy exists but is not made known, random policy setting will occur.**[7]

It is important to create a uniformity of policy format. In the Hubbard management technology, the policy is printed in green ink on white paper, distinguishing it from all other orders, directives, etc. In any case, the effect desired is that when employees receive a policy, it is immediately recognizable and given the importance and attention it deserves.

---

6   Hubbard, Policy Letter of 6 December 1970, Personnel Series 13, *Management Series.*

7   See note #6 above.

An example of policy format:

To: All Personnel
From: Jack Johnson

JOHNSON MARKETING COMPANY POLICY
June 16, 2004

Customer Service

When answering the phone, etc.

Jack Johnson
Executive Director

As policy is derived from successful actions, we'd want to consistently examine successful actions—what are or were they? One could make a list and convert them to policies.

Policy set must also create agreement. This means getting agreement on the polices through good two-way communication with those who receive it. One would want to ensure that they actually received the policy. And, if they did get it, did they read it? And even if they read it, did they understand it? If they understood it, did they agree with it? When you issue policies, there has to be a way to get feedback on the above key points.

One way to ensure that such agreement is obtained is to have a cover page on the policy being issued. It would have the name of the employee, their position in the company, the name of the policy, and an attestation which indicates that the policy was received, that it was read, and understood and agreed upon:

Sample:

> To: All Personnel
>
> From: Executive Director
>
> Date: June 20, 2007
>
> Name of policy _____
>
> Policy date _____
>
> The following filled in by recipient:
>
> Name of employee _____
>
> Position _____
>
> Date policy received _____
>
> I have read the policy. _____
> (initials)
>
> I understand the policy. _____
> (initials)
>
> I can/will implement the policy. _____
> (initials)
>
> Signed _____

If one is in agreement with the purposes of the company, and as policy promotes those purposes, they'll agree with policy and follow it exactly.

RANDOM POLICY

There is also the phenomenon of random policy. There is a good way to find "random policy."

> **Group surveys of "What policy are you operating on?" can reveal random policy.**
>
> **All bugged (halted) projects can be surveyed for illegal policy and cleaned up and gotten going again.[8]**

These data about policy, if executed properly, would send the stats of any company or an individual out the roof!

> **The most senior organizational policies there are follow:**
>
> **1.   NEVER solve the problem any junior presents to you. NEVER, NEVER, NEVER, NEVER, NEVER, NEVER.**
>
> **2.   ALWAYS investigate for the true cause of the trouble. ALWAYS, ALWAYS, ALWAYS, ALWAYS, ALWAYS, ALWAYS.**
>
> **3.   SOLVE only the problem you find after very careful investigation of the whole matter and after you have examined all possible causes of the problem.**
>
> **4.   NEVER solve a problem that has already been solved in general policy.**
>
> **5.   IF someone thinks the policy is wrong or is itself the source of the problem, then (a) he or she must be made to fully read the policy, (b) demonstrate what it is supposed to solve, (c) look over the problem he or she thinks the policy is wrong on to find the actual causes of the problem he or she is trying to solve.[9]**

---

8 Hubbard, Policy Letter of 6 December 1970.

9 Hubbard, "Problems," Policy Letter of 23 April 1965, *Organization Executive Course.*

He re-emphasizes the above as well with:

> **NEVER act on a junior's data until you have fully investigated the situation.**

> **ALWAYS investigate until you find the basic policy violation that started the problem in the first place.[10]**

The reasons for the above are made clear:

> **If you think for one moment that a staff member who won't or can't follow clear, definite policy will follow *your* orders either, you dream.**

> **The first thing you know about an off-policy-type personnel is that none of *your* instructions are being carried out either, usual or unusual. . . .**

> **You can conclude that where you have a personnel who cannot perceive the causes of things, you will have a continual spinning mess.[11]**

The above administrative truth and the following one fully describe a basic problem of management:

> **People in the organization who cannot see cause cannot solve problems, for to solve a problem one must see what is causing it![12]**

Fortunately there is a remedy:

> **1. PROVIDE GOOD POLICY.**

> **2. MAKE IT EASILY KNOWABLE.**

> **3. BE STRENUOUS IN MAKING SURE IT IS FOLLOWED.**

---

10 Hubbard, "Problems."

11 See note #10 above.

12 See note #10 above.

One can, up to a point, add policies on and on, limited only by the ability to get them known, and leave an organization or movement (a) unaffected, (b) increased in readiness to meet emergencies, or (c) crippled. The wisdom of the policy and whether or not it was a successful solution to some actually possible confusion or crisis determines whether or not it should be added or deleted.[13]

---

13 Hubbard, "The Structure of Organization, What is Policy?" Policy Letter of 13 March 1965, *Organization Executive Course.*

CHAPTER 29

PURPOSES: YOUR POWER BASE

I n arriving at one's purposes for any given activity, it is only necessary to look back at the earlier steps of the Admin Scale, especially your ideal scene (remember that the ideal scene is a **"clean statement of its purpose"**[1]).

If someone is intending to go from A to B, there must be enough courage, intention and determination to get to B, to overcome the barriers that may get in the road.

Determination to move in a given direction comes from purpose.

Do you think Albert Schweitzer decided to do what he did by sitting in his house and thinking, "Hey, you know, I got nothing to do, I think I'll go over there and help all those people in Africa"? He was determined with a purpose so strong that it overcame any and all barriers.

Without purpose, there's not enough forward thrust. And when life throws some "junk" in the way, if you don't have the courage and the basic purpose in view, when attempting to get from A to B, you're going to end up at C or D.

Why are you in the profession or industry you're in? Why are you doing it is a question that can lead you to purposes. If someone is in a job or profession to "make a few bucks" it is likely that he or she will not be in it very long (or will soon be very unhappy), as the

---

1 Hubbard, "How To Find And Establish An Ideal Scene," Policy Letter of 5 July 1970, *Management Series*.

purpose of money alone is a weak purpose. "Make a few bucks" is down at the bottom of the Admin Scale—somewhere in statistics. The purpose of the activity is much higher on the scale. And purpose leads into goals, higher yet.

PURPOSES and GOALS are at the top of the scale. The area of energy and sparks. The engine of the scale. If one has no particular goals or purposes in sight, that's drudgery. Burnout.

There should be alignment between your work and your personal purposes. A majority of millionaires became wealthy because of love of their work. They suddenly find themselves wealthy. They were so immersed in the purposes of the activity they were engaged in that they were not aware of the rewards they were accumulating.

If you don't want the drudgery, the way to get through it all is to get through to the purposes. Formulate the purposes and get them accomplished.

This area of the Admin Scale spotlights what business you are really in. It highlights the nature of your business.

Once you have isolated the purposes, it is only then necessary to move up a notch and ask why would one be involved in these purposes. This should give you a lead into goals. "If I achieved all these purposes, then what would happen?" That will help lead you into the goals.

As a further example, let's examine my own purpose as an educator.

"To educate and motivate people so that they can better achieve success." This then leads to my goal, "Saner, more productive individuals in society."

Let's review another example. A television broadcaster's purpose might have something to do with "correctly informing people so that they have an up-to-date and better understanding of what is happening in their environment." The goal might be "well-informed people who can make more accurate life decisions." For a person involved in broadcasting, that'd be pretty invigorating stuff. The broadcaster is not only getting behind the microphone and telling people what's happening, he's helping them to make judgments, to make decisions in their daily lives. That gets him up in the morning and gets him through the hassles of the day.

Yet another example: a forest ranger. His purpose might well have something to do with "protecting the perimeter of the forest from destruction (fire, mayhem, etc.)" and lead to the goal of "the preservation of our natural resources."

When you write up the goals and purposes of your area, I have found that there should be a "spark." That is to say, if you write up your goals and your purposes and you are just plain bored, it would be my opinion that either you just don't have it right or that you're in the wrong business! To be successful you must want to be in that business. You could have five or ten purposes and you could have three or four goals.

As one pins down the purposes and goals of the company, an increased enthusiasm usually occurs, a desire to produce the products of the company occurs, and a rekindled overall association with the company and its activity results.

There should be a surge of energy, some excitement!

STOPS ALL OCCUR BECAUSE OF FAILED PURPOSES.

BEHIND EVERY STOP THERE IS A FAILED PURPOSE.[1]

---

1 Hubbard, Target Series 1, Policy Letter of 14 January 1969, *Organization Executive Course.*

If one is feeling "stopped" or simply in a condition of no forward motion, the original purposes must be examined. If there is a "stop" in the forward motion, there must have been motion at one time. Therefore, to rehabilitate the motion, to get past the stop, examine the original purpose.

THERE IS A LAW ABOUT THIS—ALL YOU HAVE TO DO TO RESTORE LIFE AND ACTION IS TO REKINDLE THE FAILED PURPOSE. THE STOPS WILL AT ONCE VANISH.

That law is so powerful it would practically revive the dead!

It applies to organizations.

It applies to cities or nations. . . .

Purposes must be executed. They are something to DO.[2]

The classic alligator story illustrates the point quite well. Bill wants to build a large housing complex but there is a swamp that must be handled first. He needs to drain the swamp for the eventual housing. He begins the draining process but discovers alligators and there are problems in getting rid of the alligators due to conservation laws and other similar issues. He fixates on the alligator problem and becomes the head of the Anti-Alligator Association, etc. He loses track of the overall purpose to drain the swamp and eventually abandons his goal of new housing. Failed purpose.

PURPOSE TRAINING

The purpose of an activity in which one is involved is vital for a full understanding of why they are doing what they are doing. "This is the way you do it" may bring about instant action but it does not

---

2 Hubbard, Target Series 1.

bring about understanding. In our business consultations, we survey client staff quite a bit. "Why do you do it that way?" A common answer is: "If I didn't do it that way, my boss would really be angry." Management by consequence. That's a very low level of activity. They should be doing things because of the purpose, because they know why it needs to be done. By doing so, the "noise" in an organization, company or family can be eliminated.

THE CURE: HATTING

If you've got an area that's giving you problems, you can attack the problem by examining polices and purposes. An examination of policy and purposes is necessary to reduce stress in an area.

THE ENTURBULENCE (COMMOTION AND UPSET) IN AN ORGANIZATION IS DIRECTLY PROPORTIONAL TO THE IGNORANCE OR ABSENCE OF POLICY AND PURPOSE.[3]

Unless you give employees the full picture (and the purpose behind it by asking them, "Why do you think we do it this way?") you can't create judgment and understanding. Unless you create understanding, you're going to be developing "robots," people who come to you for solutions, people who constantly ask you what to do next. That is not effective management.

Hatting creates stability and purpose. And common purpose creates agreement.

If employees don't understand the purpose behind the actions, they are not likely to do the actions to accomplish the purpose. Purpose helps them make it their own—they own it!

---

3 Hubbard, "Organizational Enturbulence," Policy Letter of 4 October 1969, *Organization Executive Course.*

We see this in personal finance areas often. Joe is always broke, always owing money. You ask him what policies he's operating on and you're going to hear the wildest stuff you ever heard. "Well, the main policy is get to the bank before the check I sent clears." These are all his "policies." No wonder he's always behind. He doesn't have the policies of "Do not spend money that I do not have" and "Earn more than I spend."

Joe is not hatted on the rules of finances. Proper and adequate hatting is vital to productivity and success.

> LAW: BY GIVING A PERSON A POST OR POSITION HE IS SOMEWHAT STRENGTHENED AND MADE MORE CONFIDENT IN LIFE.
>
> LAW: BY LETTING A PERSON RETAIN HIS POST HE IS MADE MORE SECURE.
>
> LAW: BY HATTING[4] A PERSON HE IS GREATLY STRENGTHENED AS HE IS HELPED TO HOLD HIS POST.
>
> A basically insecure person who feels he is unable to hold his position in space is sufficiently strengthened by hatting to feel secure enough to do his job.
>
> LAW: HAVING A HAT, BEING HATTED, AND DEMONSTRATING COMPETENCE MAKES A PERSON FEEL CAPABLE OF HOLDING HIS POSITION IN SPACE AND HE BECOMES MORE STABLE, CONFIDENT IN LIFE AND MORE POWERFUL.[5]

When the office routine is becoming difficult and you're down at the bottom of the Admin Scale in "stats" and "products," trying to

---

4 Getting trained for one's job. (See footnote on page 42 for definition of "hat.")

5 Hubbard, "Why Hatting?" Policy Letter of 29 July 1971, *Management Series*.

get up to the ideal scene with no plans, not a heck of a lot of policy (and if it is, it's not being followed) and no particular goal and purposes in sight, that's drudgery—burn-out.

There's got to be enough drive at the top of this scale to get someone to persist through the problems and discouragements of the daily grind. When someone gets up in the morning and knows that this day has a lot to do with a known purpose, he can withstand a lot of the "hassles" and still get through the day, because the purpose is driving it forward.

If you wish to have more highly motivated employees with a stronger sense of participation and a stronger sense of involvement, help them to fully grasp the purpose of their positions and see to it that they are trained in them.

CHAPTER 30

THE NATURE OF GOALS

I n "An Essay on Management,"[1] Mr. Hubbard discusses the nature of goals:

> There are probably as many goals as there are men to dream them, probably more. Goals can be divided into two categories, roughly. The first would be survival goals and the second would be nonsurvival goals. Actually most goals are a combination of both, for goals are occasionally set forth solely for their appeal value, not for their actual value. One sees that the goal of a nation which directs it to conquer all other nations ends up, after occasional spurts of prosperity, in racial disaster. Such a goal is not dissimilar to the money goal of most "successful" industrialists or boards. One might call such goals acquisitive goals entailing, almost exclusively, the ownership of the MEST[2] accumulated through hard work, by others. . . .

> A survival goal then is actually only an optimum solution to existing problems, plus theta[3] enough in the dreamer to reach well beyond the casual solution. . . . It

---

1 Hubbard, "An Essay on Management," Policy Letter of 9 January 1951, *Organization Executive Course.*

2 *MEST*: "a coined word, meaning matter, energy, space and time, the physical universe." Hubbard, *Technical Dictionary.*

3 *Theta*: "the life force, life energy, divine energy, *élan vital,* or by any other name, the energy peculiar to life which acts upon material in the physical universe and animates it, mobilizes it and changes it." Hubbard, *Technical Dictionary.*

can be postulated that theta goals could bring about a much higher level of enthusiasm and vigor than the most grandly brass-banded war ever adventured upon.

EXCHANGE

The company you own or job with which you are entrusted should be looked upon as an entity in and of itself and contributed to. When doing your Admin Scale, don't make your company goals into your personal goals. The "Acme Ball Bearing Company" does not have the goal of "free time for a vacation." Keep the purposes and goals of your company or group as company or group purposes rather than personal goals.

You've got to contribute to this entity called your company or your post or hat, and make it survive. Because it survives, it gives you what you want. If you consider only your personal survival, this leads to ripping off the company's income, not making sure it survives and not ensuring it gets paid before you do. It has needs, it has requirements: rent, electricity, telephone, etc. Once it has handled its obligations, then it pays you, based upon your production to it.

Some find it hard to separate their personal wants from the group or business activity. But it is important to recognize that the exchange one receives from the company derives from one's contribution to the achievement of the company goals.

Gross Income is really the Valuable FINAL REWARD for which the VFPs are exchanged.[4]

UTILIZING THE ADMIN SCALE

You can do an Admin Scale on any subject. People who are unhappy or unproductive in life need to do an Admin Scale on their lives.

---

4 Hubbard, "Product Correction," Policy Letter of 6 April 1972, *Management Series.*

What products are they producing as a person? What statistics? What is their ideal scene as a human being? What plans and programs do they have to improve as a person based upon what policy? What are their basic purposes and goals in life? If you were to help someone do such a scale, you might very well have started him on a new life.

When doing a scale, don't get stuck or grind a particular section into the ground for hours trying to get it perfectly stated. You can start with any part of the scale. You don't have to start at the bottom or start at the top as long as you end up with all segments in alignment. And remember:

This scale is worked up and worked down UNTIL IT IS (EACH ITEM) IN FULL AGREEMENT WITH THE REMAINING ITEMS. . . .

The skill with which all these items in any activity are aligned and gotten into action is called MANAGEMENT. . . .

Groups appear slow, inefficient, unhappy, inactive or quarrelsome only when these items are not aligned, made known and coordinated.[5]

---

5 Hubbard, Policy Letter of 6 December 1970, Personnel Series 13, *Management Series*.

CHAPTER 31

LEVELS OF CAUSATION

The whole subject of the Admin Scale and its alignment is really all about the subject of being causative, making things happen. It is very causative to keep an activity expanding. And it is best done on a gradient scale. In L. Ron Hubbard's article on "causative organizations," he indicated:

> **An organization is somewhere on the scale of operating causatively. Any organization is. Of any kind.**
>
> **An organization can figure out the vital targets and push them through to completion or it can't.**
>
> **It's a gradient scale. . . .**
>
> **Thus there is a gradient scale of causativeness. It's not an absolute. One is as successful as he can CAUSE things.**[1]

And target attainment (completing the planning steps) is what achievement is all about:

> **One of the things to cause is target attainment. When somebody can push through a target to completion, he's to that degree causative.**[2]

---

1 Hubbard, "Target Series 1," Policy Letter of 14 January 1969, *Organization Executive Course.*

2 See note #1 above.

How do you know what targets to do? How do you know what are the most important areas to handle first? In the same issue, Hubbard details what it takes:

> **What it takes to make an organization go right is the intelligent assessment of what *really* needs to be done, setting these as targets, then getting them actually fully *DONE*. . . .**
>
> **Man's worst difficulty is his inability to tell the important from the unimportant. . . .**
>
> **It takes good sense to be able to survey an area and find out**
>
> 1. **What MUST be done.**
>
> 2. **What SHOULDN'T be done.**
>
> 3. **What is only desirable to be done.**
>
> 4. **What is trivial.**

The success of an organization is very much a factor of being at a position of cause, not effect.

> **An organization succeeds or fails to the degree its individual executives and staff members can measure up to being Cause. . . .**
>
> **You *can* assess the situation.**
>
> **You can drive targets home to full completion.**
>
> **Every executive and every staff member is somewhere on the scale of causativeness. And he can rise higher just by setting up the targets and plowing them through to done, done, done.**
>
> **Yes, it requires ideas. But ideas come from interested looking and sizing it all up before you set the target in the first place.**

You can even raise an organization by gradients so as not to overwhelm it. Set and make small targets. Then bigger and bigger ones.

Well, you get the idea.

It's the organization's road to causativeness.[3]

---

3 Hubbard, "Target Series 1."

CHAPTER 32

ACHIEVING SUCCESS

My basic purpose for this book aligns with my responsibility for the dissemination and impact of Mr. Hubbard's work in society.

Having worked with and for Mr. Hubbard, and having been personally trained by him on numerous occasions, I know how tirelessly and joyously L. Ron Hubbard worked for over fifty years researching the mind and spirit and the tools of management so that they could be used to make a better life for us all.

He desired the broadest use of these tools and challenged us to demonstrate our competence in its implementation.

> **Probably the reason this universe itself is considered by some as a trap, is because their Admin Scale is out.**
>
> **And the only reason this universe is sometimes a trial, is because no one published its Admin Scale in the first place. . . .** [1]

The Admin Scale is an important and very powerful tool with which to play the games of life.

---

1 Hubbard, Policy Letter of 6 December 1970, Personnel Series 13, *Management Series.*

INDEX

expansion of business (con't)
organizing for, 63–65
over-expansion, 67
physical laws governing, 69
targets or quotas, 115–116
uncontrolled expansion, 70
via sub-products, 67–72

F
failure
acceptance of, 79–80
no such thing as, 81, 92
reasonableness and, 83–84
reasons or excuses given for, 80–83
See also, "no option" theory
financial management, 73–74

G
goals
in Admin Scale, 3
company versus personal, 168-169
defined, 6, 134
nature of, 167-169
product delivery and, 17
survival and non-survival, 167-168
theta goals, 167-168
time factors, 168
gradient scale, 132, 171
graphs
and importance of scale, 111–112
justifying, 100–101
multiple graphs for comparison, 108–110
See also statistics
groups
functioning, xvii
internal pressure, 27
staff income and pay, 28
survival of and individual members, 74–75
See also personnel; teamwork

H
hard work, as opposed to effort, 10
hatting, 163-165
havingness, defined, 55
How to Live Though an Executive **(Hubbard)**, xviii, 1
Hubbard Colleges of Administration
founding of worldwide, xviii
Hubbard, L. Ron
administer (defined), 19
on Administrative Scale of Importance, 134–135
on administrative skill, 12
on being interested, 61–62
on demand for income, 74, 106
on dismissal of employees, 76–77
on dreams for the future, xvii
on conditions of exchange, 25–28
on the exchange principle, 19–20
on expansion formula, 115
expansion maxims, 68–69
on false or true data, 16
on fixed ideas, 122
goal (defined), 6, 133
on goals, 167-169
on graphs and scale, 111
on hatting, 163-164
ideal scene (defined), 5, 117
on justifying a graph, 100–101
Law of the Omitted Data, 16, 125
management (defined), 7, 141
on managerial effectiveness, xix
on no such thing as failure, 81
orders (defined), 135
on organizational enturbulence, 163
on organizational failure, 71–72
on organizational knowledge, xvii
on *over*expansion, 67–70
planning (defined), 134
plans (defined), 5, 131, 134
on policy authorization, 153